SONGWRITING SUCCESS

HOW TO WRITE SONGS FOR FUN AND (MAYBE) PROFIT

SONGWRITING SUCCESS

HOW TO WRITE SONGS FOR FUN AND (MAYBE) PROFIT

An introduction to the art and business
of songwriting by one struggling singer–songwriter
for the aid and comfort of other strugglers.

MICHAEL LYDON

Routledge
New York • London

29 West 35th Street
New York, NY 10001
www.routledge-ny.com

Published in Great Britain by
Routledge
11 New Fetter Lane
London EC4P 4EE
www.routledge.co.uk

Copyright © 2004 Michael Lydon
Routledge is an imprint of the Taylor & Francis Group.
Music examples by Steve Cohen
Graphic examples by Michelle Drollette
CD recorded at Batcave Studio, NYC. Engineer: Gary Dorfman
CD edited and mastered at MacIntyre Music, NYC. Engineer: Reed Robins

Printed in the United States of America on acid-free paper.
Book design and typesetting: Jack Donner, BookType

10 9 8 7 6 5 4 3 2 1

Library of Congress Cataloging-in-Publication Data

Lydon, Michael.
  Songwriting success : how to write songs for fun and (maybe) profit : an introduction to the art and business of songwriting by one struggling singer-songwriter for the aid and comfort of other strugglers / Michael Lydon.
     p. cm.
  ISBN 0-415-96929-8 (pb : alk. paper)
  1. Popular music—Writing and publishing. I. Title.
  MT67.L93 2004
  782.42'13—dc22
                                                              2003026492

for Ellen, my muse, my partner, my wife;
and for Martha Sanders, Dave Lewis, Ed Fennell, Ron Wolfe,
Zane Massey, Rudy Lawless, and Terry Newman,
an inner few of the many guys and gals I've played with—
thank you for your generous, soulful music.

Contents

part II: The Business of Songwriting

CD Tracks:

Track One: Chord Structures Part I

Track Two: Singing

Track Three: Song Forms

Track Four: Melody

Track Five: Rhythm

Track Six: Chord Structures Part II

Track Seven: Refinements

Track Eight: Guitar/Vocal Demo: "Let's Live Our Love Again"

Track Nine: Fully Produced Demo: "Rain Drip Dropping"

Introduction

So you want to write songs? Join the club!

The Lord must have told the Adam and Eve of songwriters, "Be fruitful and multiply." So many of us minstrels are wandering the earth these days trying to be heard that I'd like to tell a few thousand of you, "Give me a break; quit and become accountants." Fat chance!

Joking aside, songwriters face constant competition. In every city and town, down the block in every neighborhood, other guys and gals are writing songs, and many of those guys and gals are good, really good. So, even if you are good, you may never win fame and fortune. For years your masterpieces may be heard by a circle little wider than your family and friends, earning only a fickle trickle that keeps you in guitar strings and groceries. While a few lucky bums, who are no damn better than you, are racking in the big bucks, Grammies, and covers by superstars! Maddening!

I'll try my best to steer you toward the big bucks, Grammies, and superstar covers, but since songwriting is a tough business, I also caution you: Don't let making money be your only goal. If you do, you'll most likely burn out from frustration. Don't give up, but let this first lesson sink in: enjoy your work for the pleasure it gives you—that may be the only reward you're gonna get.

Writing songs, fortunately, delivers rich rewards. For creative challenges, lifelong learning, and just plain fun, nothing beats writing, singing, and playing your own songs. Looking back at my own thirty-year career, I remember the birthdays of new songs as golden moments in my life. These were days when I walked about on a little pink cloud, a new melody playing about my ears, my mind happily darting this way and that for the perfect rhyme, the perfect finishing phrase. I've had low moments too, of course, but living through them has given me three cornerstones:

1. Love of Craft—Enjoy songwriting; strive to improve your skills; respect songwriting's traditions as you innovate.
2. Love of Self—Believe in your songwriting; write songs to tell the truth about feelings and ideas that matter to you.
3. Love of Other People—Use songwriting to share your joys and sorrows with other human beings.

Ground your work on these cornerstones, and you will continue to write songs and to enjoy writing songs, no matter how well or badly you do in the marketplace.

Actually, the best marketing tip of all is to make craft, self-expression, and reaching other people your deepest goals. Songs that become hits and then long-lived standards are, without exception, well-crafted songs that express true feelings and touch many hearts.

Let's get to work. I don't know how much you know already, but this book, I think, will give fresh knowledge to beginners, ear-opening new ideas to intermediates, and will remind more advanced writers of principles none of us can afford to forget.

Michael Lydon

A Note on the CD

Each track on the accompanying CD explores the chapters on music, with me playing many of the examples and connecting them with a bit of talk. The examples played are marked in the book by a CD icon.

For best results, first read each chapter and try the examples yourself. Then follow the CD with the book before you, your instrument and voice at the ready.

part I

The Art of Songwriting

chapter 1

Deep Background

Songwriting requires so many music and word skills that beginners often feel overwhelmed. Shall I write the music first or the lyrics? How can I play well enough to play the songs I want to write? How can I make song demos when I sound like a bullfrog every time I sing? What do you mean there's no rhyme for silver?

The only way to quiet such worries is to face them one by one, and that's what we're going to do: break the art of songwriting into units we can tackle one at a time.

But before getting down to specifics, let's open ourselves to songwriting at its broadest reach. Let's realize how songs and music already permeate our lives. If you're anything like me, and I figure you are, you know hundreds if not thousands of songs: lullabies you heard in your crib, hymns you heard in church, songs you've danced to or romanced to or sung along with, songs that made you laugh, songs that made you cry, songs from movies, songs from Muzak, songs from other centuries and from countries and peoples all around the world. We humans cannot close our ears, so, if blessed with good hearing, we can't avoid taking in whatever "airs" the breezes bring us. If you think of it, we are all swimming in an ocean of songs.

Do think of it. Now is the time to raise your lifelong immersion in songs from the back to the front of your mind. Think of any song you know from "Three Blind Mice" to "You Are My Sunshine," from Irving Berlin's "Blue Skies" to Lennon and McCartney's "A Hard Day's Night." How does the song go? Sing a bit of it. How does it make you feel? What makes the song memorable? "Mary had a little lamb, its fleece was white as snow." Why has that become an immortal ditty, sung by millions generation after generation? Why do we humans love songs? What do songs give us? What do songs tell us about life, about ourselves? How do songs reach our hearts?

You may not find answers to such questions, but ask them, and you'll begin to sense the mysterious power of songs, these fluid sounds that surround and connect us. Your songs are your response to this ocean of music, little ships that you'll launch on its bosom, hoping that, like the old favorites the ocean brought you, they will steer past shoals of indifference and storms of fashion and still be sailing around the world long after you are gone.

The song ocean has a history as old as humankind and far older than that if we consider the many songs of nature: the songs of birds and of bees, of wolves and of whales, of fire, wind, and rain. Every culture boasts of its storied past in odes that speak in voices unique to each culture: *The Iliad* and *The Odyssey* are songs and so are the Psalms and *Beowulf.* The modern songs of Europe and the West spring from medieval roots: from solemn Gregorian chants intoned in monasteries, from gaudy passion plays, operas really, that retold the story of Christ with music sacred and profane. Modern songs also spring from the romantic ballads of troubadours who wandered from castle to castle, forever pining for their lady fair and forever hoping that singing sad songs about her would win them a roof over their heads and a bite to eat beside a roaring fire. "Ring around the rosey, pocket full of posies, ashes, ashes, all fall down," perhaps the oldest European song still widely known, has survived as a nursery rhyme but began in the 14th century as a morbid satire about the Black Death: "Ashes, ashes, all fall down" mocked the many plague victims who sneezed before they died.

Become a song historian and you'll never find time to write songs, but do find ways to taste these song traditions. If you see a flyer on a church bulletin board for a Gregorian chant concert, go. If a Baroque music group performs at a nearby college, go. Get to the library or a record store and pick up a handful of CDs of Renaissance chansons or Monteverdi operas. Move up through the centuries: Palestrina, Vivaldi, Bach, Handel, Haydn, Mozart, Beethoven, Rossini, Berlioz, and Brahms—they all wrote songs. Find one of the widely available volumes of 17th and 18th century Italian songs like "Caro mio Ben" (My Dear One) by Giordani, songs still loved by singers everywhere for the lilting beauty of their melodies. The pristine, passionate songs (*lieder* in German) of Schubert and Schumann will repay a lifetime's exploration. Arias by Puccini, Bizet, and Verdi are not quite songs, being long and freeform, but many opera melodies, like "La donna e mobile" (Women are Fickle) and "The Toreador Song," became instant pop hits that millions can still hum today.

American song grew in the 19th century from Appalachian fiddle tunes, African slave spirituals, and Stephen Foster's ballads and minstrel songs. Scott Joplin's rags, "Maple Leaf Rag" and "The Entertainer" among them, made a bridge to the syncopated, bluesy songs by 20th-century greats Irving Berlin, Jerome Kern, Fats Waller, George Gershwin, Duke Ellington, Cole Porter, Harold Arlen, Richard Rodgers and Lorenz Hart, Leonard Bernstein, and Stephen Sondheim. This Manhattan school of city songwriters was one of many. Hank Williams and Johnny Cash wrote country songs in Nashville; Burt Bacharach and Hal David wrote suburban songs in Los Angeles. Muddy Waters and John Lee Hooker wrote blues songs; Chuck Berry and Buddy Holly wrote rock 'n' roll songs; Charlie Parker and Dizzy Gillespie wrote jazz songs; Bob Dylan wrote protest songs. In the 1960s when Britishers John Lennon and Paul McCartney and Mick Jagger and Keith Richards began writing songs as good as the American originals they copied, the American song became the music of the global village. Four decades later that American song style—its words and melodies, sounds and rhythms—still dominates the globe-circling world of popular music.

Several of these songwriting schools you may know well. Some you may like; others you may actively dislike. Now is the time to dump your dislikes, to expand your horizons, to dip into traditions and genres you're not familiar with or think you don't care for. Listen in a restaurant or elevator—what songs are playing on the Muzak? Go slowly back and forth across the radio dial, AM and FM, staying on each new station for an hour or more. Get CDs of artists you've heard of but never heard. Don't let your prejudices get in your way. Every song that becomes popular must contain some value, must answer some human need. If you can't stand a song that other people enjoy, listen again and ask yourself, "Why do they love it? Why do I hate it?" Songs you must push yourself to like may never become favorites, but for a few spins at least, sit back and listen with an open mind. Their creators are hopeful guys and gals like you, remember; give them the benefit of the doubt. I guarantee that from a few of those strangers you'll learn much you can apply to your own music.

We swim in many oceans: the ocean of headline news, wars and treaties, presidents and princes; the ocean of domestic life, Mr. Jones losing his job, Betty and Bob having a baby, Grandma not getting on so well since Grandpa died. We swim in the ocean of ongoing nature, our world spinning around the sun, our lovely moon shining silver in the night-blue sky, summer turning into fall, winter into spring, days of rain following days of fair weather. Most intimately, we live in the ocean of human emotion, billions of us living on earth, our lives endlessly interplaying and overlapping, each one of us inside a rainbow of hopes and fears, each one of us yearning to know and love others, to have others know and love us.

These oceans are too vast to comprehend, yet to write good songs, you must study them as best you can. From these oceans your songs will grow. Songs are about Betty and Bob and having babies, about summer afternoons and autumn sunsets, about soldiers marching off to war, about being young and growing old, about every shade of love that shimmers in our hearts. To know these oceans well enough to write about them, you must first, last, and always:

observe life. Take long walks along country lanes and along city streets. Keep your eyes and ears open, your mind alert, your memory taking notes. Some mornings when you wake up, write down your dreams. When with family and friends, forget about being the life of the party; instead, sit back, listen, and watch how the others get and give attention. You won't always sit on the sidelines, of course; you'll fall in and out of love, cry your eyes out when your mother dies, get a new job and move cross country, etc. Everything you observe and experience, painful or pleasurable, will feed your songs.

Often, as you write you won't care about this deep background, whether it is madrigals or moonlight. Instead, you'll be madly focused on whether you need another repeat of the chorus or should the next chord be an A minor or an A seventh? Yet developing an ongoing openness to music and nature and human emotion will enrich your work and connect your songs more closely to your life and the lives of others. Also, as a mysterious benefit, the deep background will often suggest answers to nitpicking questions of craft. More than once when I've gotten twisted up in writing an intricate lyric, a song fragment like "Your cheating heart will tell on you," has flashed into my brain, reminding me that there's nothing better than simplicity.

chapter 2
Reading Music

Some self-taught songwriters, and some great ones, don't read music, but these exceptions will not excuse you from becoming a reading musician yourself. If you hope to build a professional career, you must read music. You should be able, overnight if not instantly, to sing and play a reasonable facsimile of what's written on the paper in front of you.

Fortunately, the written music that songwriters need to read is simpler than the scores conductors read to lead an orchestra through Beethoven's Fifth. Most pop songs are written in lead sheet form, one line of melody and chord symbols:

Example 1

Sometimes there is a simple accompanying instrument part:

Example 2

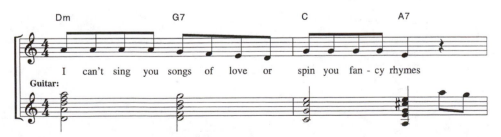

Many good books lay out the key and time signature, note and time value basics of music notation—and the Appendix lists a few—so I'm assuming that you know or can learn about the staff with its G clef that has the notes E–G–B–D–F (Every Good Boy Deserves Fun) on the five lines and F–A–C–E on the four spaces:

Example 3

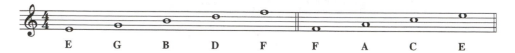

What helps me see past the complexity is to remember that Western music notation is a graph. The horizontal axis represents time; the vertical axis represents pitch (how high or low the tone). A melody moving forward in time and going up and down in pitch makes a curve on the graph:

Music notation can become complex; any musician would be initially daunted by a passage like this from a piano piece by Brahms:

Example 4

What helps me see past the complexity is to remember that Western music notation is a graph. The horizontal axis represents time; the vertical axis represents pitch (how high or low the tone). A melody moving forward in time and going up and down in pitch makes a curve on the graph:

Example 5

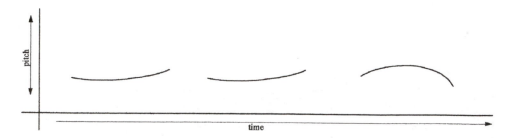

That curve is easy enough to read; try singing it on la-la. Written music plots that curve on the lines and spaces of the staff:

Example 6

So, when reading music, look for the melodic curve that the notes describe; you'll find it easier to see the shape of the music that way rather than by reading the notes one by one. You may be reading along one day and be terrified by a cluster of sixteenth notes:

Example 7

Your fingers or vocal cords will twist into knots unless you see that those sixteenth notes are just a final flurry before a big curve comes to rest:

Example 8

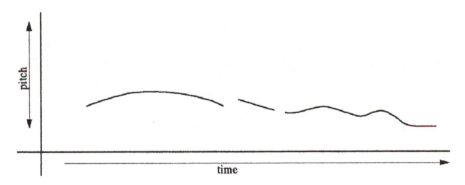

Don't knock yourself if you find reading and playing from written music difficult to master. Every musician I know wants to improve his or her reading skills. Be patient, but keep at it. Reading music will open up treasure troves of music, will let you play, in your own way, the mighty works of Bach and Beethoven, the songs of Gershwin and Ellington, any music that you've ever loved but thought, "Gee, I could never figure out how it goes."

Here are four reading tips from my own hard-won experience:

- Take the time to isolate the rhythm of what you are reading from its
  tones. Read the rhythm of this melody from a Chopin ballad:

Example 9

Now read it minus the ups and downs of pitch:

Example 10

When you can tap that out with your hand or sing it "la-la" in a
monotone, then you'll be more prepared to add the ups and downs of
the curve.
- Likewise, isolate the notes that create two distinct curves: the *melody*, or
  top line of the music, and the *bass line*, or bottom line of the music. For
  example, turn this classical guitar étude by Tarrega:

Example 11

into this, playing each line separately:

Example 12

The melody tends to be the most prominent line in a piece of music, the line listeners hear distinctly and think, "That's the song." The bass line, though heard less consciously, anchors a piece of music; it's the low, slow line on which the high, quick melody dances. If you can get the feeling of the melody and bass line, middle lines, which once made no sense, will soon fall into place.

- When reading, play slowly enough that you can keep going despite mistakes. Let your eye follow the written music, moving ahead at a steady tempo past all your stumbles. If you keep collapsing at one point, stop, examine, and practice that passage, then try to reintegrate it into the ongoing flow. The goal is to stay on the pulse of the music as you read, no matter how tangled your fingers get. Stopping for every goof breaks up the momentum that could carry you over the rough spots. Instead, play slowly but keep going. A mistake you make one time you'll not repeat the next time around. Soon the pulse of the music will relax and untangle your fingers, and a passage that was once a choppy mess will be a smooth, coherent statement.

- Sightread all the time! Make reading new music part of your daily routine. You'll learn most from the best composers, whether Mozart or Brahms, Cole Porter or Richard Rodgers, but almost any music will do. Get a songbook from the library or a hymnal from church and open it to any page. You don't need to play at first, just read the music. What key is the piece in? What's the time signature? What does the melody line look like? What's its range? Tap out its rhythm. Then try playing the piece; start by playing the bass line. Play the piece once or twice through, repeating any section that strikes your fancy. When you get tired or frustrated, go on to another piece or another unit of your routine. The idea is not to play the new piece perfectly, but to make a habit of looking at fresh music and bringing it to life. Some music you sightread you'll never look at again; some you'll play for the rest of your life.

Writing Music

As well as reading music, you will, of course, be writing music, notating the chords and melodies of your songs on paper. Writing music with clear, easy-to-read quarter rests and dotted sixteenth notes takes practice. Put the time in and learn to do so; the Appendix lists books with all you need to know. Yes, you may often use computer programs that need only a few clicks to turn out elegant perfection, but computers break or aren't there when you need them. Every working musician must be able to write music legibly. Some composition teachers, I'm told, would have flunked Beethoven because his manuscripts were messy. A bit extreme, perhaps, but the professors have a point. If you want other people to read your music, make it easy to read.

Write in pencil until the final draft; we all make mistakes and need to rewrite. "The eraser is the most-used end of my pencil," says a composer pal of mine. A rich black #1 pencil makes a bold impression and photocopies well. When possible, put four measures on one line; so much music is written in eight-bar or other even-numbered forms that four-bars-a-line gives you a good chance that your song sections will end at the end of a line. Here's a sample of my hand, which many musicians on gigs and at sessions have found to be on the good side of adequate:

Example 13

chapter 3

Chord Structures—Part I

When listeners like a song, they sing the melody—the single dancing line that carries the words. Melody matters, to be sure, but for the songwriter, *chord structure* matters equally. However pretty its melody, a little song house will only stand up if its chord structure is sound, if the roof and walls stand plumb on a strong foundation.

Modern chord structures are built on the Western musical system of twelve tones. In this system, each tone has its own key, each key has its own eight-step scale, and each scale step has its own chord. This system—studied under the names *music theory*, *harmony*, or *tonality*—is complex, but if you want to write songs, you must put in the time and effort to understand, if not its furthest reaches, at least harmony's central principles.

The principles of harmony are based on physical facts. To grasp how the facts and principles connect, we need to make an excursion into acoustics, the science of sound. I'll make this excursion as brief as possible, but bear with me; you'll always use, and always rely on, what we discuss in the next few pages.

Let's start with the sound of a single musical body: your vocal cords, a guitar or piano string, an oboe's air column. If you sing "Ahhh," pluck a string, or blow into an oboe with your fingers stopping certain holes, a *tone* results. A tone is a single definite sound that we can name (e.g., *A*, *B*, or *C*), and define by its *frequency*, how many times it vibrates per second. Today *A* is the universal name of the tone 440 cycles per second. Because each tone is a compact sound unit, tones can be used as bricks in building a piece of music, and melodies can progress confidently from one tone to another:

Example 14

Mar - y   had   a   lit - tle   lamb

We could call the tone music's irreducible element but for an irreducible mystery: every tone contains many tones. When we pluck a single string, complex vibration results. The loudest vibration is that of the whole string:

Example 15 Track One

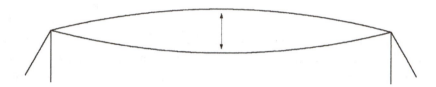

This is the *fundamental* tone of the string, let's say *A*. At the same time all the *parts* of the string are vibrating too, the halves, the thirds, fourths, fifths and so on up to the hundredths and beyond, each creating its own *partial* or *overtone*. Prove this to yourself: pluck a taut string and listen to its tone. Pluck again and touch the string lightly at the half, third, and quarter points. Listen to the faint higher tones that remain. One plucked string creates not one tone, but a shimmering composite of many tones:

Example 16 Track One

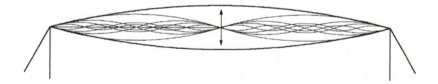

Analyzing the many tones in one soon leads to a crucial fact: half the string vibrates twice as fast as the whole, and its tone, though higher, sounds enough like the fundamental to be called the same name. If the fundamental is *A*, the half-string tone is also *A*. When men, women, and children sing "Happy Birthday" together, the high voices sing the melody on tones twice the frequency of the low voices, and all blend in apparent unison. As half the string sounds *A,* so does the fourth of the string, the eighth, and so on, and strings twice or four times as long sound lower *A*s. So we have *A* at 55, 110, and 220 cps as well as *A* at 440, 880, and 1760 cps.

This repetition of like-tones gives music a structure we can see on the music graph. We can use two like-tones as borders between which melody can swoop and curve:

Example 17 Track One

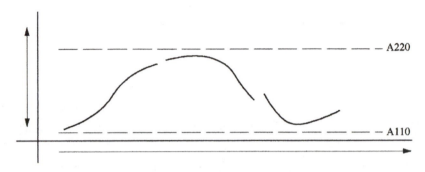

Or we can a place a like-tone between two other like-tones and let the melody curve to the borders and return home to the center:

Example 18

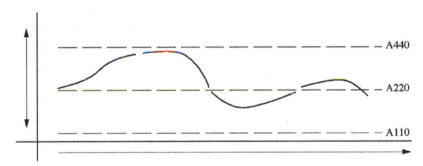

Let's go one step further: What tone does a third of the string create? Verify this yourself, but I assure you that this overtone, vibrating three times faster than fundamental, does not sound like the fundamental. It's part of, but distinct from, the composite. This new tone repeats at a sixth and a ninth of the string, and it can be used structurally just like the repeating fundamentals. Between *A* 440 and *A* 880, for example, lies this new tone at 660 cps. Since it springs from the single string, the new tone makes a natural stopping place for a melody moving between two fundamentals:

Example 19 Track One

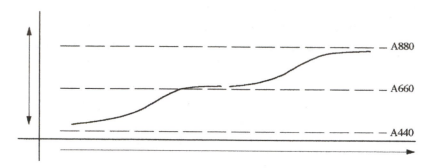

Before going on to give the Western names for these tones and their relationships, I remind you that the phenomena the names describe—many tones in one—are facts of life utterly untouched by who plucks the string or when, whether Homer plucking his lyre or you strumming your guitar today. Musicians call the many tones in one tone the *chord of nature*, and the name rings true: we can use and shape, but not change, this raw material. Any string, plucked any time, brings the chord of nature to life.

In common parlance, musicians call the fundamental *do*. The *do re mi fa sol la ti do* scale crosses the interval between the fundamental and first overtone. The third of the string creates the tone *sol*, the fifth step of the scale. In more formal terms, *do* is called the *tonic* and *sol* the *dominant*. From the tonic all other tones spring; the dominant dominates the interval between two tonics. Think of a staircase with a wide landing between two floors, and you'll start to get a sense of how tonic and dominant give structure to music:

Example 20

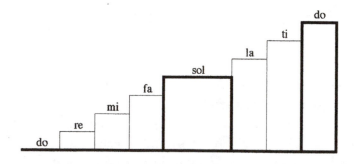

Examples of tonic and dominant combined and alternated abound in the music of all times and cultures; to cite a hundred or a thousand examples would still be to pick at random. Here are a handful: the melody of "O Tannenbaum" (Oh Christmas Tree) starts on the dominant and leaps straight to the tonic; tonic and dominant sounded together create the wail of the Scottish bagpipes and the drone of the Indian sitar; the four strings of the violin family of instruments (violin, viola, cello, and bass viol) are tuned so that each string is dominant to the string beside it.

This brings us to our first principle of chord structure:

Moving back and forth from tonic to dominant is the biggest, strongest, and most common tonal movement in music.

To begin sensing the natural rightness of this pendulum-like swing between tonic and dominant, start singing do-sol-do-sol-do up and down, over and over. The sooner you can get the sound and feel of tonic-dominant movement into your ears and mind, the better prepared you'll be to sense the structure of nearly every song.

To continue, about the time of Bach (1685–1750), Western musicians discovered that if they adjusted, or *tempered*, the chord of nature, they could fit its overtones into a twelve-tone *chromatic scale*. This is a scale easily heard by playing one key after another up or down a piano keyboard, or moving fret-by-fret up a guitar neck:

Example 21

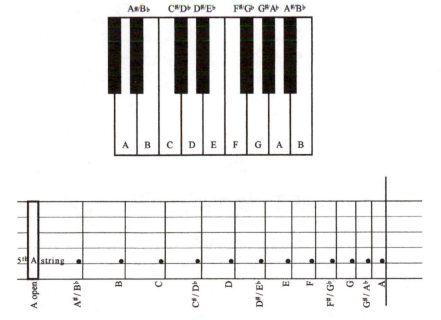

On that tempered scale Western musicians built a comprehensive and interlocked system in which any of the twelve tones can be a tonic. When one tone is the tonic, the music is in the *key* of that tone. Each key has its own eight-tone scale drawn from the twelve tones. That is why we call the *do* to *do* interval an *octave*.

How are these keys related? They are related by tonic and dominant. If we are in one key and wish to go to its closest relative, we go to the key built on the dominant of the original tonic. Thus the key of C, with no sharps or flats, is followed by the key of C's dominant, G, with one sharp, then by the key of D, G's dominant, with two sharps, then A, D's dominant, with three sharps, and so on, eventually looping back through the flats to C. In each scale the dominant is the fifth step (*do re mi fa sol*), so musicians call moving from tonic to dominant to new tonic "going around the circle of fifths." This superb tonal system, still in use around the world after two and a half centuries, is a great, graceful wheel of resonant, related tones, turning through time:

Example 22

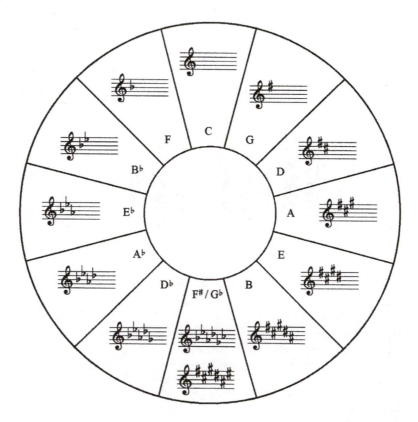

Let's take one last listen to our single string. Having found the tones of the whole, half, and third of the string (and of the fourth as a repeat of the half), what tone does the fifth of the string create? A fifth of a string tuned to *A* 110 sounds a tone at 550 cps, which lies between *A* 440 and its dominant at 660 cps:

Example 23 Track one

Musicians call this new tone, *mi* on the major scale, the *mediant* because it falls roughly in the middle between tonic and dominant. When the three tones are played together, they become a chord called a *triad*. A *major triad* occurs when the mediant is tempered slightly higher than the pitch that occurs in the chord of nature; a *minor triad* occurs when tempered slightly lower. If one tone is a brick, a triad is a stout, three-tiered cinderblock, a condensed version of a string's three primary overtones:

Example 24 Track One

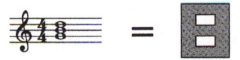

Musicians build triads on each step of the twelve major and twelve minor scales. Look the others up in your music theory book. Here, as is commonly done, I'll let the C major scale and its triads stand for the rest, naming each chord with a Roman numeral:

Example 25

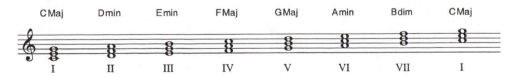

These triads are named *scale tone triads* because they use only tones in the scale of C major. Though we are calling these chords separate entities, note that they have many linking tones: the I triad (C–E–G) has a G in it, linking it to the V chord; the IV triad (F–A–C) has a C, linking it to the I; the II (D–F–A) has F–A together just like IV (F–A–C). We needn't say more about scale tone chords now, but remember the name. We'll come back to these essential tools in *Chord Structures—Part II*.

If the big movement in music is from tonic to dominant and back, then what are the most important chords? That's right, the tonic and dominant chords, the I and the V chords. This brings us to the second basic principle of chord structure:

Balancing the tonic and dominant chords in nearly any symmetrical sequence will create a stable structure for a song.

The old folk song "Down in the Valley" is a fine example of a song that supports its melody with tonic and dominant chords that change on pivotal rhymes:

Example 26 Track One

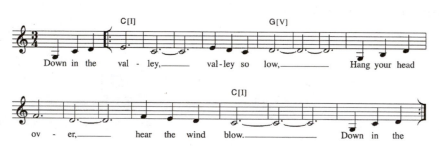

Identical tonic-dominant structures can support many different melodies, or, to put it another way, you can write many songs using the same balanced sequence of I and V chords. Here are two simple songs that I often play for children because the natural alternation from tonic to dominant, the same in both, helps the kids get the songs right away:

Example 27

ZOOM, ZOOM

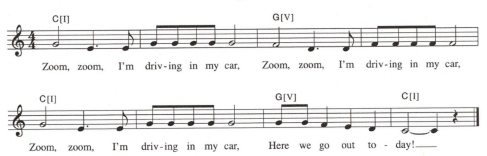

Zoom, zoom, I'm driv-ing in my car, Zoom, zoom, I'm driv-ing in my car,

Zoom, zoom, I'm driv-ing in my car, Here we go out to - day!——

Example 28 Track One

LET'S SHAKE HANDS!

Let's shake hands and say hel - lo, Let's shake hands and say hel - lo,

Let's shake hands and say hel - lo, I'm so glad to see you!

Now you see why we took that excursion through the acoustics of vibrating strings and their overtones. Grasping that science gives us a handle on a simple, useful songwriting method based on music's deepest principles: strum the I and V chords in the key you know best at an easygoing tempo, sing a melody on la-la, and see what words pop into your head. Countless songwriters have used that method for centuries, and it has given birth to countless gems.

One further element of song structure needs to be discussed here. In the key of C major, as we've seen, the I chord is the C major triad, the V chord the G major triad. Now ask yourself: what chord has C as its V chord? Well, lay out the C major scale, calling C V for the moment, and you'll soon see that F, IV in the C scale, has C as its dominant:

Example 29

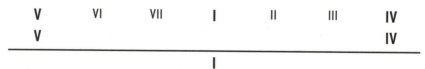

			[I	II	III	IV	V]
C	D	E	F	G	A	B	C
I	II	III	IV	V	VI	VII	I

The major triad build on the IVth step of the scale—the chord that has I as its V—is the third most important chord in song structure. Musicians call the IV chord the *subdominant*. The name accurately suggests the chord's role just below the dominant in structural strength. Now that we've included it, we can add the IV chord to the second principle and come up with the third principle of chord structure:

Balancing the tonic, dominant, and subdominant chords in nearly any symmetrical sequence will create a stable structure for a song.

I find it helpful to think of I, IV, V set not in a row as above but with I set in the center and IV and V four scale steps away on either side balanced like kids on a seesaw:

Example 30

V	VI	VII	I	II	III	IV
V						IV

I

Try this next little melody and see how natural it feels for the tones to run from the I up and down to the IV and V and back home to the center:

Example 31 Track One

These I, IV, and V chords are the famous "three chords" of so many folk, blues, country, and rock songs. Glance at any songbook of old American tunes like "Michael, Row the Boat Ashore," or songs by Hank Williams, Woody Guthrie, Chuck Berry, or Bob Dylan, and above the written music, there will be a parade of C, F, and G chord symbols in one sequence or another. Play "She'll Be Comin' 'Round the Mountain":

Example 32

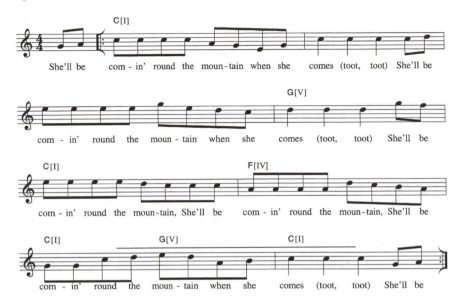

Not every song is written in the key of C, of course, but if we look we can find the I, IV, V structure in the new key. For, if the following is true,

Example 33

I	IV	V
C	F	G

then the same relationships exist in the other eleven keys. Here are the I, IV, and V chords in four other commonly used keys:

Example 34

I	IV	V
A	D	E
D	G	A
E	A	B
G	C	D

Now that you can see the same structure in any key, you can play "She'll Be Comin' 'Round the Mountain" in whatever key best suits your voice. Just think, "Wherever I've played a C chord, I'll play the I chord in the new key. For the F chords, I'll play the IV, for the Gs, I'll play the V."

Getting the feel and sound of I, IV, V chord structures in your ears is of paramount importance. Play this structure that I've used for several songs:

Example 35 Track One

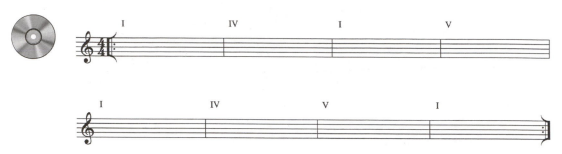

I strongly suggest you play this structure in the five keys listed above, singing la-la or your own words in any melody you think of. Do the same with the classic three-chord blues structure:

Example 36 Track One

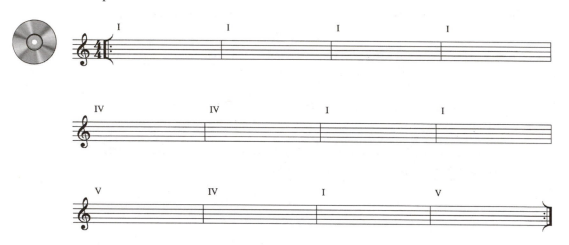

We'll come back to more complex chord structures later, but before leaving structure for the moment, I'll remind you that, no matter how far you go in music, you will always find structures based on I, IV, and V. Tonic, dominant, and subdominant—chords rooted in the fundamental and first overtones of any vibrating body—create the essential skeleton of Bach cantatas, Mozart symphonies, elegant jazz and Broadway songs, as well as folk classics like "This Land is Your Land." Anytime a complex song baffles you, step back and ask yourself, "Which chords express the I–IV–V building blocks? Which chords are more decorative?" Looking for I–IV–V structure will also help your reading. See these notes in the next example not as random tones, but as a zigzag run up the scale from I to V:

Example 37

chapter 4

Playing, Singing, and Performing

Some songwriters never want to be heard out of their studios. They know enough music to bang through a song and get it on paper, but they gladly leave the rest to professional players and singers. Sixty years ago that was the norm; songwriters wrote on battered uprights in smoky offices, then sold their songs to Tin Pan Alley publishers who found the singers to sing them.

The norm changed in the 1950s and 60s when rock 'n' roll, blues, and country songwriting exploded, and writer-performers like Chuck Berry, Buddy Holly, Bob Dylan, Lennon and McCartney, and Jagger and Richards came to the fore. Most songwriters today perform regularly. They enjoy being in front of an audience; they also know that unless they sing and play their songs in public, the chance that anyone else will is nearly zero. This is the age of the singer–songwriter, a solo performer who can, entertainingly, accompany him or herself singing original songs.

What this means for you is that you must work on your playing, singing, and performing skills. Let's look at each skill in that order.

Playing an Instrument

The piano and guitar are the singer–songwriter's classic instruments. If you have not started studying one of them already, start now.

Learning to play a musical instrument well is one of the great lifetime challenges any human can take on, and those who rise to the challenge are widely and rightly admired. Legend tells how great masters love their instruments, how they search endlessly for more resonant tone and greater depths of musical understanding. The image of cellist Pablo Casals practicing, practicing, practicing well into his nineties formed my youthful picture of a maestro's dedication. Tenor saxophonist Ben Webster put it this way, "I'm one of those guys, I'll be playing that horn 'til they close the lid on me."

You may not want to become a virtuoso, and even if you did, you might practice eight hours a day for decades and never reach your goal. God gives brilliant instrumental gifts only to a few. Fortunately this poses no problem for us songwriters. We only need to play well enough to carry our songs and put a frame around our singing.

Yet there's a double rub. First, to play common-garden accompaniment takes years of intensely applied study. Second, to reach that low goal, you must reach for the high one. People who don't play music, I think, may not understand that competent playing is a hell of a lot harder than it looks. There is no way to play an instrument at a professional level and also study it lackadaisically. You have to work on your instrument, put in long hours, use your best brain-power. Your instrument will demand all you can give it of your patience, your stamina, and your willingness, your eagerness, to pick yourself up after the latest appalling failure and try, try again. Talk about blood, sweat, and tears! After you've done thirty years of solitary in the practice room, you'll know what I'm talking about.

If you love your instrument, however, those hours will be among the happiest in your life. You'll float in grooves of pure sensual delight, fight dogged battles to hard-won triumphs, and feel the thrilling pleasure of breaking through to new levels of understanding. Month by month your eurekas will add up to a proud awareness of increasing ability. At your next performance you'll happily sense, "Oh, that scale is so easy now, and yes, the people are reacting more, they're more in tune with me."

The path each player takes to playing a musical instrument is unique, but nearly all paths share three elements: *routine, teachers,* and *fellow musicians*.

Routine

When I began studying guitar in 1971, I realized this was a subject I'd never get to the bottom of. No one ever does. How would I tackle a job I knew I'd never finish? Soon I knew the answer: by working at it like a miner digging coal. Every day the miner goes to work, swings his pickax against the rock face, and makes his few inches of progress. Then he goes home, eats, and sleeps. In the morning, rain or shine, and even though he'd rather stay in bed, he takes his pickax back to the mine and starts swinging at the rocks again. That's how you learn to play a musical instrument, by making practice a daily routine that you stick to no matter what else is happening in your life.

If you can find time for four hours of practice a day or more, great. Most of us have to make do with less, but here's the rule: A little practice every day is better than chunks of practice widely separated. I tell my students that if they wait for the perfect rainy Saturday afternoon when the house is quiet, that afternoon will never come, but if they grab spare half-hours, those half-hours will stretch because the fun of music will keep them going overtime. Think of practice time as a savings bank. Putting a few dollars in every week will add up faster than waiting for the $100 that's always needed for something else.

Make what you do in your daily practice also routine (and by daily, I don't mean every single day—take a few holidays!). Divide your practice sessions into sections. Start with an opening warm-up followed by technical exercises. Then do a spot of sight-reading before going on to working up new or refreshing old repertoire. Make a routine that suits you, but do find a routine. Don't start strumming the same old songs the same old way, then noodle some lick you remember vaguely from a record, play a scale or two, then start a song and stop where you always stop because the rhythm is tricky. Disorganized dabbling leads to dead ends.

Systematic study, on the other hand, takes you where you want to go. Set yourself goals and push toward them in logical steps. Go to the library or a music store and find two or three good books on theory, technique, or style that suit your level. Take them home, start on page one, and work your way through them. When you finish these books, get more that will take you to new levels. If guitar is your instrument, play Mauro Giuliani's superb series of exercises still in use after two hundred years; if piano, play a similar series by Carl Czerny. Find the music in the exercises as you play them again and again. Play them with a metronome, gradually increasing the tempos.

Look back at the I–IV–V song at the end of the last chapter, and play it in all twelve keys, going around the circle of fifths. Pick a song you already know and learn it in new keys. If a book uses a term like "augmented chord" or "Lydian mode" that you don't understand, don't skip over it. Instead, do what you need to do to find out what the term means, then hammer that knowledge home by using augmented chords in a new song or writing a melody in the Lydian mode.

Routine can frame and support any course of study and give you benchmarks to measure your progress. Habit, I've found, is a powerful force. As bad habits can pull you down, good habits can lift you up further than you'd dream possible. Make practicing an enjoyable habit in your life.

Teachers

Every musician needs a teacher, one at a minimum. Over the years and for various needs, a musician may need up to a dozen teachers or more. You can learn a lot of music from books, and I encourage self-reliance, but I cannot imagine anyone learning to play an instrument without substantial hands-on guidance from a more experienced player. The principles of structure in the last chapter, for example, have subtleties that slip away when a novice tries to grasp them. "Doing what comes naturally" on the key or fretboard will more likely cramp your hands with unconscious tension than give you the "natural" technique you crave.

Starting out, I couldn't afford to pay for lessons, so I stole what I needed from books browsed on the sly in music stores. I did okay, but linking up with a teacher earlier would have sped my progress. By now I've studied with many fine teachers, principally voice with Julia Wortman and guitar with Pasquale Bianculli. I've understood many musical concepts and passed many technical roadblocks only because Miss Wortman and Pat have stuck with marble-headed me while I struggled with tone production and scale fingering, or have patiently explained umpteen times, "Open your mouth for the high notes," or, "No, Michael, keep your second finger on that fifth string B through *both* chords."

Get a teacher. Who? That depends on whom you can find. Any American community larger than a hamlet will have at least a handful of guitar and piano teachers. Not every teacher will be right for you. Take your time to find someone whom you trust, whom you can connect with, and whom you can learn from. On the other hand, don't reject a teacher too quickly if that teacher pushes you in directions you aren't familiar with. Maybe the teacher knows what you need better than you do. If your big goal is to write modern pop songs, then you may not want a teacher to take you too deep into the classical tradition, but don't turn down any chance to learn music from your instrument's distinguished past.

Good teachers will help you set up your routine and suggest music to read, concerts to attend, and records to listen to. Perhaps most importantly, your teachers will cheer you on through times when your upward learning curve turns discouragingly flat. A healthy teacher–student relationship can become a delightful partnership and a vigorous friendship. Pat and I seem to laugh as much as we work. The teacher leads; the student follows; but both are equal, both lifelong students of music's mysteries. The best teachers always say how much they learn from their students, and good students often become teachers. Thus music nourishes itself, one generation passing the fruits of its labors on to generations coming up.

Fellow musicians

We must work lonely hours in the practice room to learn music, but music is not a solitary art form. Music needs people, the more the merrier. Humans sharing together, feeling together, talking together—music is a means to those ends. We musicians share and feel and talk intimately with our audiences. How much more intimately, more deliciously, can we share, feel, and talk with our fellow musicians?

So, as soon as you can play two chords, start looking for other guys and gals to play with. No, don't wait "until you're good enough." Go now. Somebody out there is dying to play with you. Put your two little sparks together and make a fire.

Join the choir at your church. Put up a notice on a music store bulletin board, "Songwriter–guitarist looking to swap songs with a congenial soul." Let your friends and workmates know you are playing. I bet you'll find one of them plays a little too and that she'll be glad to get together some Saturday afternoon. Studying music at a school gives you a big advantage in meeting other musicians at your level. If you're taking private piano or guitar lessons, sign up for group classes in composition and theory. Try out for a school ensemble, whether the jazz band or a chamber group. Making music with other people is one of life's great joys. Why delay?

I know why . . . because "we're all sensitive people," as Marvin Gaye wrote in a fine song. Opening yourself musically to another player can be nerve-wracking. "He'll sound good; I'll sound lousy," that's the basic worry. From that bad seed can blossom nightmarish feelings of inadequacy that cause atrocious playing and red-faced, run-away-and-hide embarrassment. I've got scars, believe me.

Still, don't be shy. Get out there. So what if you goof up? Dying of embarrassment seldom proves fatal. Overcome your fear of playing with others by realizing, "These cats are as nervous as I am." Music is an emotional matter for every musician, a precious, private state where hopes and fears come nakedly to the surface. Admitting your own nervousness with a grin will likely get a comradely "Me too" in response. Don't pretend to know more than you know. If somebody says, "F-sharp minor flat five," and you go, "Huh?" then ask a few questions, make a few notes, and check it out when you get home. If your playing partner starts running away with the tempos or picking all the keys, speak up: "Hey, let's slow this baby down a tad," or, "Sorry, but that key is too high for me." Yes, you'll run into a few pompous jerks and get a few rejections. Big deal. That's likely if you stick your nose out in any direction.

Far more common than jerks and rejections will be the cheerful guys and gals you'll enjoy jamming with once, twice, or a hundred times. Make playing with new people another good habit and your initial nervousness will fade. You'll learn something from everyone you play with. Some who know more than you will become informal teachers; to others, you'll teach a few tricks of your own. A few will become friends, and one may turn out to be the other half of a hot new duo looking for gigs.

In sum, the joys of playing music with fellow musicians far outweigh the agonies. Getting into a groove with a goodhearted bunch, everybody listening and responding to each other, one stepping out to solo then falling back to support others, the music, by the osmosis of mutual understanding, building to crescendos, ebbing away to pianissimo endings—ask any player and they'll tell you: there's no fun like it in this world.

Singing

As you must learn to play, you must learn to sing. Many pop music hopefuls forget that singing too demands disciplined study. They spend tons of time and money on their instruments but won't make a similar investment in their voices. Afraid that vocal lessons will kill their "natural sound," they squawk at the microphone year after year, telling themselves, "Well, Bob Dylan sounds awful, too."

Bob Dylan sounds great, in fact. He may never have studied voice, but years of passionate singing have honed his voice into a flexible, expressive instrument, a voice recognized around the world. Rough and ready on-the-job-training may do the same for you, but offstage hours practicing singing will greatly improve your odds.

Everything I've said about learning an instrument applies to learning to sing—the lifelong challenge, the patient routine. Why? Because your voice is an instrument, an instrument made of your own body, a flesh and blood air-cello that uses your diaphragm to pump air past your taut vocal cords, whose delicate vibrations get amplified by the resonating chambers of your ribcage, mouth, nose, and sinus cavities. Most humans get a standard issue voice at birth, serviceable but undistinguished. Your job is to customize that voice into your own Stradivarius that can coordinate the actions of many muscles and body parts, produce clear, resonant tones across at least an octave and a half, and on which you can rely to sing, expressively, any song you like.

An instrument like that isn't built overnight. Only after eight years of study did I feel I had a voice, dependable if not brilliant. By then I'd learned that if I kept it fresh with daily exercise and a weekly lesson, I could use my voice as I used my guitar. I knew my vocal range as I knew my guitar neck, knew where my tone was meatiest, where it grew thin. I knew how to study a song, how to find the key where it lay best for my voice, how to find my own phrasing of the melody, my own interpretation of the lyric. Since reaching that plateau a dozen-plus years ago, I've continued the same study routine, polishing and burnishing my voice, still feeling like a beginner.

The big difference between singing and playing an instrument? Singing feels even more vulnerable. Players can hide behind their instruments, use them as diverting props, scapegoats for goofs—"Man, the B-flat key was sticking." It's just you, head-to-toe you, when you sing. Singers call difficult high notes "exposed" because that's how they feel singing them, like escapees spread-eagled in a prison spotlight. If the eyes are the windows of the soul, the voice is its loudspeaker, one that can tell more about us than we'd like to reveal. When I sing, I feel sure that listeners can read my every thought and feeling. Singing a wildly wrong note at the end of a verse, thus ruining my entry into the chorus, can keep me squirming for days.

All musicians talk through their instruments, but drummers don't play paradiddles to ask the price of potatoes. Singers build their instrument from the same mental and physical apparatus we use for speech. An amalgam of thought, word, and emotion, speech stands at the core of our humanity. Each of our voices is unique. What we say is often less important than how we say it. Friends and family can hear our changing moods in the slightest changes of our voices. From sarcastic snorts to soft sighs, sobs to chuckles, giggles, and guffaws, from tones high and loud to low and soft, wide-awake to sleepy, gentle to rough, indifferent to curious, pleading to commanding, caressing to scorning—in the course of one ordinary day we color our speech with a rainbow of vocal tints and shadings. While retaining speech's primordial power and sensitivity, singing amplifies its tones, intensifies its hues, widens its range, and broadens its appeal with melody, rhythm, and harmony. No one wonder great singers stir great multitudes.

The voice is too close, too "us," to be seen objectively; learning to sing on your own or from a book is impossible. Get a teacher. Good voice teachers are not as plentiful as guitar and piano teachers, but if you call a music school in your town or the music department of a nearby college, you'll find one. Yes, you are planning on singing pop not *Pagliacci*, but go first, not to a pop or jazz vocal coach, but to a teacher who can ground you in the classic vocal technique called *bel canto*, "beautiful singing" in Italian. Without limiting you to any one style, bel canto will give your voice a stable core that you can shade toward jazz, pop, blues, or any way you like. Bel canto values a smoothly connected vocal line (think Frank Sinatra) and achieves it by daily singing legato scales and exercises. Here are two that I do, moving up and down across my range in half steps, singing the classic singing syllables, *do, re, mi, fa, la* and *ti*:

Example 38 Track Two

Note that the second exercise is the I chord going up and the V dominant chord coming down. Listen for that as you sing the exercise.

Your teacher will guide you through these and similar exercises, making suggestions as you go. Then, when deemed ready, you'll start on songs. Your first song may be as simple as "Row, Row, Row Your Boat," but don't scorn "Row, Row, Row." It has a lot to teach. Look how the melody of the first phrase climbs from *do* to *sol*, how the second phrase leaps to high *do,* then tumbles back down the octave to low *do*:

Example 39 Track Two

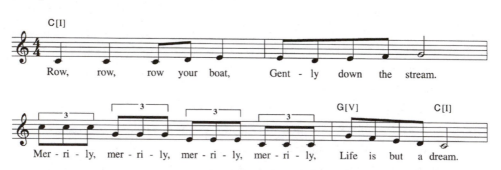

Sing "Row, Row" in different keys to test the limits of your range. Sing it as a round with your teacher, and suddenly you're singing harmony. Sing the "row, row's" softly, swell on "gently down the stream," climax with "merrily, merrily," then let your voice fall with the melody to the end. That's a fine way to begin shaping a melodic line. Let laughter enter your voice on the "merrily,"

a hint of regret on "Life is but a dream," and you've begun putting emotion into your voice.

When you first sing this or any melody, try it on la-la, then add the lyric to the vocal flow you've already established. It's fine to give your voice rough expressive textures, but don't let your textures push you out of tune. Be tough on yourself about singing blurred approximations of a melody; pick your notes out one-by-one on your guitar or keyboard to make sure you know what you're singing. Sing your own songs with your teacher, and sing great songs from vocal music's vast repertoire. Generations of singers have loved songs like "Caro Mio Ben," "Drink to Me Only With Thine Eyes," "Who is Sylvia," "Silent Night," "Danny Boy," "O Sole Mio," "Old Man River," "La Vie En Rose," and "Body and Soul" because they are beautiful and because, being beautiful, they are fun to sing and wonderful for your voice. Following the curves, swoops, and well-prepared leaps of a lovely melody, and expressing the feeling of its tones and words, are the best exercises you can give your voice. Learn a few of these ever-popular chestnuts to perform and to keep your voice healthy and supple.

Here are a few tips from my experience:

- Take big breaths. A quick but full breath that swells up your chest, back, and tummy cures many a vocal problem, makes singing in tune easy, and makes crisp diction no problem. A smooth sing-breathe-sing-breathe rhythm sets up relaxed and natural phrasing.

- Open your mouth. You've seen pictures of opera singers with their lips stretched wide, every molar visible, chins down to their chests. You seldom need to go that far singing pop, but you cannot sing any style well with a clenched jaw.

- Smile. Smile while you're singing, and instantly your voice will relax and your singing improve. Smile mechanically if need be. The simple act of turning your lips upward will suggest happy thoughts, and your grin will soon be genuine. Smiles convey humor, intelligence, and affection. They open you up to your audience and your audience up to you. Smile, even if wryly, on sad songs. You may have the blues, but you're glad that you're singing.

- Sing lightly. All trained singers know to work their bodies, not their throats. You need vigorously to expand and contract your diaphragm, chest, and back muscles because they support the breath that vibrates your vocal cords, but keep everything in the throat and head airy and relaxed. Singing feels more like yawning than shouting. "You are pressing on your larynx," Miss Wortman has told me a million times when she heard me grinding out tones I should have let free. Throat tension pushes your tones out of tune, tires your voice, and can lead to persistent hoarseness and even calluses on your cords from too rough wear. If your voice feels heavy and dull, think, "Light, light, light," as another vocal coach tells her students, always adding, "But your support must be like a rock."

- Sing at a comfortable volume. Trying to sing too loud can start the nasty tension, tone-grinding, out-of-tune chain reaction. Your singing volume will grow as your coordination, relaxation, and strength grow. Microphones mean there is no need to bellow.

- Vary your volume. Let the melody and the lyric tell you where to sing whispered pianissimos and where window-rattling fortissimos. Varying your volume establishes a rhythm of contrasting moods. Declare forcibly, comment reflectively; out to the audience, into yourself. Singers who sing whole songs at one volume remind me of waiters reciting long lists of menu specials. I order the soup du jour just to shut them up.

- Enunciate. Singing teachers can drive you crazy by saying they didn't hear you hummm your m's or zizzz your z's. However maddening, they are probably right. Listen to them, listen to yourself, and practice until you can sound each vowel and consonant of your lyrics distinctly. What may feel over-enunciated to you as you sing, audiences will hear as passionate plainspeaking. They may know what you mean if you sing, "I luh you, gir," but your careless diction will suggest careless emotions: how much do you really care for her if you can't sing out, "I love you, girl" loud and clear?

- Keep your eyes open. Closing your eyes as you sing may help you concentrate and may seem soulful, but do it sparingly. Your baby blues (or browns or greens) are powerful communicators. Use them with your face and body to support and extend the feelings in your voice.

- Sing harmony. Singer–songwriters mostly sing solo, but take any chance you get to sing with other people. Singing harmony can do wonders for singing in tune, finding a melody's ebbs and swells, and smoothing out rough patches in your voice.

How do you learn to sing harmony? Strum a simple folk song, and you'll find it easy to sing variants of the original melody. Get together with a pal or two and try improvising harmonies for "Down in the Valley" or "Swing Low, Sweet Chariot." Sing whatever comes easily at first, but over time put thought into it. The basic rule: you can sing any tone that fits the chord you are playing. So if you sing "Down in the Valley" in the key of C, for instance, you could sing the whole lyric on G, the *sol* of the key, which appears in the I triad (C, E, G) and in the V triad (G, B, D). That might sound dull on its own, but lovely when combined with another voice singing the melody. From such simple beginnings, you can work out increasingly intricate parts:

Example 40 Track Two

Down in the val - ley,_____ val - ley so low,_____ Hang your head ov - er,_____ hear the wind blow._____ Down in the

- Sing! The more you sing, the better you will sing, and the more your voice will become YOU—a flexible instrument you can use to express the wide range of emotions you feel inside and that you hope to convey to the world.

Performing

Playing and singing before people is an art in itself, an art both inspiring and terrifying.

The only way to learn to perform is to perform; experience is performing's great and only true teacher. Invite your instrument and voice teachers to your performances. They will surely give you excellent feedback, but they'll come as friends and colleagues, not teachers. Classes in acting, dance, comedy, or public speaking will teach you much about talking and moving before an audience. Take them if you can, but you'll learn more from what happens to *you* as *you* move and talk before an audience than from what a teacher tells you about the experience. If you haven't started performing already, start now. Last one in is a rotten egg!

From this day forward, take every chance you can to get up in front of people and sing and play your songs. Playing for pals makes a good start. Invite friends and family to your living room for a musical evening. Always perform at your teacher's student recitals. As soon as possible, get out into the world and perform for people you don't know. You need to learn how to win over a room full of strangers. Start looking, and, at a ferns-and-quiche coffeeshop in the student part of town, the stuffy basement of the Methodist church, or the community center Rec Room on nights when Bingo is off, you'll find someone running an open mike or hoot night or amateur hour where, if you show up at the right time and put your name on a list with the other hopefuls, you'll get to do your three to five songs. You'll go through a million nutty emotions:

"I'm a genius." or "Oh no, what is the next chord?" or "Is that girl laughing at me? "Then you'll take your smattering of applause and go off, feeling bruised, exultant, and dying to get back up there and do it again, better.

My partner Ellen Mandel and I first stepped on stage in the early 1970s at such a place, the Seventh Seal Coffeehouse at the Lutheran campus center in Berkeley, California. To get a good Saturday night spot at the Seal, we had to get there an hour before sign-up time, and week after week we did. Six months later we got hired for a Friday night, seven dollars and fifty cents, two forty-minute sets. Not much but, we figured, "Now we're pros." We've never looked back. Make your debut in a homey place like the Seventh Seal (though even in the smallest club you'll find, as we did, a few backstage backstabbers). When you have a few performances under your belt, start looking further. From bulletin boards and grapevine gossip, you'll hear about other open mikes at bigger, classier clubs across town or in the next town. Scout them out, and when you're ready, jump to the next level.

In your early days, fear of failure may loom as a high barrier. The agonies of stagefright, knees quaking, stomach heaving—and the even more exquisite tortures of crashing and burning onstage—you get confused, forget your new song's second verse, one person laughs, you stop, everybody laughs—are truly soul-searing moments. "I *died* out there," performers say after a flop, and they're not joking. How to cure flop sweat? Commit yourself to performing as you commit yourself to practicing. Make each performance an experimental step in an ongoing process, "one more chance to try to get it right," said blues singer Joe Williams. So you bombed? Well, you're not the first, and you won't be the last. Admit your mistakes, but don't beat yourself up about them. Learn from your mistakes. Where, why, and how you goofed reveal points that need practice. Give those weak spots chunks of time and attention in the week ahead. Then climb back on the horse. Next time, you'll knock them dead.

Perform. Just do it. On the other hand, don't wing your performances. Be prepared. Write out a set list and stick to it. "The best adlibs are the ones you make up the night before," said George Burns. Tune up *before* you go on. When your time comes, walk out, smile, say, "Hello, glad to be here," and get your first song rolling. If you make a mistake, smile. If you get totally lost, fake and keep going. If you have to stop to get straight, do so with an "Oops!" and a grin, and start over. Bow at the end, leave the stage briskly. That night, don't listen to negative criticism. You are too vulnerable. Over the next few days, though, get feedback from people you trust. Pour everything you learn into your next performance.

Perform more than your own songs. Sing any well-known songs, whether "S' Wonderful" or "Wabash Cannonball," your crowd will be glad to hear.

Familiar songs will win over strangers. You'll learn from the inside what makes classic songs work, a priceless lesson for your own writing. Go further afield: read a poem or a short story at the open mike or try out for a musical at your local community theater. If you've always let other people make the show-and-tell presentations at school, your job, or the PTA, try a few yourself. However different these forms of performance, they share countless common elements. What you learn from one you can apply to the others.

Persona

By performing again and again, singing the same songs, connecting them with the same patter, and making small and large adjustments as you learn, you will begin to develop your *persona*, the concentrated essence of you that will become your performance vehicle, your overall instrument. What makes up a performer's persona is a subtle matter. Let's look at the long, slow process by which it grows into a stable yet flexible tool.

Stepping out to perform changes the dynamic of ordinary social interaction. Here's a group in conversation, all listening, all responding, each giving and receiving similar amounts of talk and gesture, each in turn a momentary focus of attention:

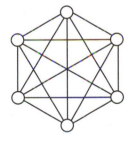

When one person steps out to perform, the lines of energy shift dramatically:

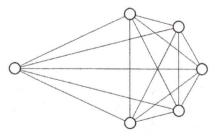

Performer and audience are still a group but now a group divided. One faces many; many face one. Stepping into the light accentuates the performer's individuality. Pulling together to watch from the dark accentuates the audience's anonymity.

To you, the performer, this eternal theater moment means: *You* are the distinct individual in the light. The many in the dark are watching *you*. You've stepped out from the many, but you still want to converse and interact with them. They sit quietly, waiting for you to make the first move.

What will you do? How will you act toward your audience, connect with them? Who will you be to them? Now that many are focusing on little you, *who are you*?

Every performer must answer these questions, and the sum of the answers is that performer's persona. Think of any well-known singer–songwriter, Chuck Berry, Willie Nelson, Bob Dylan, Paul Simon, Dolly Parton, Joni Mitchell, Bruce Springsteen, or Elvis Costello. The mental image you can form for each is their persona, the image that he or she created by answering, in an untold number of performances, the questions that face you, "Who am I?" and "What am I going to do?"

Your persona will be unique, but like all performers, you'll build it on two foundations: you and audience response to you.

As you prepare for your next performance (and as you write your next song), delve into yourself a bit. Where are you from? What's your ethnic background? Was your family big or small, rich or poor, or in-between? What do you like or dislike about yourself? About other people? Any hobbies, quirks, or passions? What do you wear to look your best? What makes you laugh, makes you cry, makes you mad, touches your heart, turns you on? Any big ideas you long to share with the world? Whatever such questions stir up inside of you, that's the raw material of your persona.

Start sharing this precious you-stuff with your audience. Actors must play characters and follow scripts, but we singer–songwriters are free to be our natural selves on stage, to sing what we please, say what we please, and dress as we please. In and between your songs, you can tell audiences much about your folks and hometown, your long-lost and newfound loves, your hopes and fears. The point is not to tell your life story in boring blow-by-blow, but to open yourself to the audience, to let them know you by the way you stand and move, by the clothes you wear and how you do your hair. Your accent and your tones of voice, your sense of humor and your sincerity, the styles of the songs you sing, the melodies, rhythms, and harmonies you play, all of these are elements of your persona, the wavelength you broadcast on, radio station WYOU.

Building your persona on yourself has one cardinal rule: Tell the truth about yourself. Yes, you may embroider or exaggerate aspects of your story for comic or dramatic effect, but you must base your persona on the true you, whoever that may turn out to be. I can't imagine anything more exhausting than lugging around the alien burden of a false persona, always afraid its flimsy facade might crack and expose the me I want to hide. A true persona, in contrast, fits like Willie Nelson's persona fits him, a public self organically connected to your private self, a second skin that will change as you change and last as long as you last with only occasional dusting and polishing to keep it up-to-date.

Now to the second foundation: audience response to you. As you present yourself on stage, the audience will respond across a wide gamut from uproarious applause to stony silence. To this response, you must listen like a cat poised by a mouse hole, your ears cocked for every shade of meaning in every sound, each laugh or sigh, cheer or boo. Audience response is your onstage lifeline, telling you which song or story to stretch, which to cut short. Audience response is your bread and butter. Your success will depend on how well you can read that response and turn it in your favor.

Here's the catch though. You may think you've got your persona together and know how to put it over, but, come showtime, the audience may disagree. "No," they'll tell you with thin applause here and cheers somewhere else, "That's not your persona. You think you're a ballad singer, but we like your rockers better. You sing like Tina Turner, but you're dressed like Patti Smith. Enough about your damn childhood, sing the next song already. Yeah, that song about your old boyfriend was funny, but your political barbs—*boring*!"

Negative audience response can come as a rude surprise. Every performer has stormed off stage spluttering, "There I was singing about Betty leaving me, and this creep at a front table yawned in my face, *yawned in my face*!" Yet, tough as it may be to accept, the audience, like the customer, is never wrong. Exceptions exist, of course, and I'm not recommending that you compromise your principles or cave to the crowd. The performer–audience relationship is a dialogue, remember. When talking with friends, you wouldn't change your mind just because someone disagreed with you. So keep singing your ballads, keep telling your political jokes, keep trying new strategies to get your point of view across. You may be playing the wrong club. If you try a club more uptown or more downtown, fancier or funkier, the audience may love your ballads and jokes.

I still advise listening to your audience. Work with them; meet them halfway. Don't lose sight of your big goals, but be willing to adjust the tactics you use to reach them. You are singing and writing songs to communicate with people, not to be, as I heard someone say on a sitcom, "All alone in Rightville."

Let's say your audience loves one of your songs which you think is only fair, and they hate one you think is great. Which one do you feature? The song they love, of course. Maybe they're hearing something in it that you don't, even though you wrote it. Maybe something about your favorite song doesn't suit you. No problem. Drop that song from your set list and start plugging it to another singer.

Having said much on a subject about which little can be learned second hand, I'll close with two hints passed down by generations of performers:

- Leave them wanting more. There is no escaping the truth of this ancient maxim. Audiences can be amazingly tolerant of inept work, but give them a performance that wanders on and on with no end in sight, and they will first get restless, then annoyed, and progress rapidly to seething dislike. Control your stage-hog impulses. Don't overstay your welcome. Trim your set of needless repetitions and fillers. A tight twenty minutes is always better than a loose half-hour. First, precision communicates more than sloppiness, and second, a tight twenty is much more likely to get you rebooked to do another tight twenty next week.
- Be bold. Faint heart ne'er won fair audience. Make every performance an expansion of yourself and an expanding experience for your audience. Stretch. Experiment. Reach out as far as you can, and then reach again. "Give me a place to stand, and I will move the world," said Archimedes. Take your stand on stage and do likewise.

chapter 5

Lyrics—Part I

The melody, harmony, and rhythm of a song communicate with music; the lyrics of a song communicate with words. This verbal–nonverbal combo gives songs their powerful one–two punch on our hearts and minds. Songs tell us all what words can and can't say in a single breath.

Words, of course, have a music all their own. First, last, and always, words are sounds. We speak words over a wide gamut from high pitches to low, and many words have customary pitch levels that are hard to change. Try saying "teeny" in a deep voice or "rotund" in a squeaky voice, and you'll see what I mean. Words set up strong rhythms, from the staccato rat-a-tat-tat of one syllable words—"the cat ate the mouse in the house"—to the legato flow of multi-syllable words—telephone, afternoon, comfortable—that build to and fall from accented climaxes—un-be-LIEV-a-ble. Putting "the em-PHA-sis on the wrong syl-LA-ble," as my mother used to say, can change a word beyond recognition. Speaking mouth-filling words with gusto—frankincense, rambunctious, multitudinous—takes us halfway to singing, and as soon as we string a few words together in a phrase or sentence, we have a melody that can be lighthearted and silly:

> … what I had said, if said to a tigress about a tiger of which she was fond, would have made her—the tigress I mean—hit the ceiling.
>
> —P. G. Wodehouse

or grave and portentous:

> Four score and seven years ago our forefathers brought forth upon on this continent, a new nation, conceived in Liberty, and dedicated to the proposition that all men are created equal.
>
> —Abraham Lincoln

If words had only tones and rhythms, using them in songs would be easy; we'd string together pretty words just for their musical sounds. But words also have meanings. Unless you're writing a nonsense song, you can't use any old words in a lyric. You must use words that will mean something to other people. Even these nonsense lyrics from the 1940s, "Mairzy doats and dozy doats / And liddle lamzy divey" can be deciphered into "Mares eat oats and does eat oats / And little lambs eat ivy."

How to balance word music and word meaning in our lyrics is songwriting's million-dollar question, a question with answers ultimately so personal that no hard and fast rules are possible.

Every songwriter tries to match music and meaning, to make the sound of the words suit and suggest what we are saying. Many different words can convey the same thought. Our job is to find the most musical combination. To give an extreme example, we could describe a new child in the family as an:

elastic male infant

or as a:

bouncing baby boy

The first sounds too neutral, too cold, to be song-like. The second conjures up a robust, red-faced little fellow we'd gladly sing about.

Be willing, therefore, to review the words that first come to mind when writing a lyric and consider other wordings that may convey your meaning more musically. "Every night I'm crying over you," "I'm crying every night over you," "I'm crying my eyes out over you," or "Can't sleep for crying over you." Which one works best will depend on your song's melody and rhythm and your own taste, but don't accept rough drafts. Keep shaping your lyric until the words fit your music like a glove.

Poets have been matching word music and word meaning for centuries, and they long ago named many language devices that they use to help them do so. That series of b's in "bouncing baby boy," for example, is called *alliteration*, a series of words that start with the same sound, and a most useful device it is. You'll find alliteration in countless lyrics, often in titles ("Where or When," "Dancing in the Dark," and "Bewitched, Bothered, and Bewildered") because the repeated sounds make the phrase easy to remember. So if you first scribble down, "I lost my darling in Mississippi," try rewriting it into, "I lost my love in Louisiana."

Rhyme is the most powerful and best-known word device of all. Rhyme occurs when ending lines have words that sound alike. Take this example from a sonnet by Shakespeare:

> But if the while I think on thee, dear friend,
> All losses are restored and sorrows end.

and this from "Yankee Doodle":

> Yankee Doodle went to town, riding on a pony,
> Stuck a feather in his cap and called it macaroni.

Rhyme depends not just on sound-sameness but on the rhythm that brings us the same sound on similar beats.

> I wanna go home,
> Why did I roam?

is a better rhyme than:

> I wanna go home,
> Why did I ever think it would be fun to roam?

Some lyricists insist that rhyme must be perfect, as in two identical ending sounds like "friend-end," but I disagree. Yes, perfect rhymes are preferable, but for pop songs sung in today's down-to-earth English, there's no harm in rhyming "more (mo')" and "go" as so many blues lyricists have done, or in matching a singular and a plural as Jimmy Van Heusen did with "Polka dots and moonbeams / Sparkled on a pug-nosed dream," or in fudging similar small differences as Gus Kahn did in "Making Whoopee" when he wrote, "He's washing dishes and baby clothes / He's so ambitious he even sews." In "You Don't Know How Cute You Are," I wrote, "You can go back to Eve, but you better believe / You got Godiva beat in a breeze." The test of an imperfect rhyme is in the singing. If you can make the rhyme roll off your tongue so easily that the audience accepts it, fine. If not, keep looking.

Struggling to find words that rhyme can be maddening but is well worth the work. A good rhyme adds a whammy to a lyric that no other device delivers. From the moment the first rhyming word sounds, audience suspense starts to build: "What will rhyme with that?" Land on the original yet inevitable second rhyming word, and their suspense will resolve in delightful discovery. A clever rhyme has a built-in smile. Take this one from Cole Porter's "Brush Up Your Shakespeare":

If your blonde won't respond when you flatter 'er,
Tell her what Tony told Cleopatterer.

Rhyme matters so much to lyric writing that I urge you to get a rhyming dictionary. One day when you're stuck, a focused search for words that rhyme with "match" may get you unstuck. On another day, idle page-flipping will give you fresh ideas.

Here's one rhyming trick of the trade: end your lines with easy-to-rhyme words. Glancing recently over a book of lyrics by great writers like Frank Loesser, Lorenz Hart, and Sammy Cahn, I noticed that "flatter 'er -Cleopatterer" rhymes are the exception. Though all the writers have wide vocabularies, they use the same rhymes over and over again: "you-through-blue," "way-day-stay," "nights-lights-sights," not to mention good old "June-moon-croon." Why? Because these clever wordsmiths put hard-to-rhyme words like "Republican," "calamity," and "cheerfully" in the middle of their lines and put the easy words with the big fat vowels at the end. So if, let's say, you're writing a lyric about flowers, end your lines with "rose" (chose, those, pose, nose, doze, goes) or "lily" (Millie, filly, dilly, silly, Billy), and put "nasturtium" (???) in the middle. You may think one wording such as, "Fall flowers bloom all red and orange" is pure genius, but unless you flip that around to "orange and red," you'll never find a rhyme.

On the other hand, the end of a line isn't the only place for your rhyme. Master lyricists delight in devising *interior rhymes*, rhymes that fall somewhere in the middle. Note Ira Gershwin's early interior rhyme in these two lines and the final rhyme with its big-beat three syllables before the end:

I *love all* the many *charms* about you
Above all, I want my *arms* about you.

Remember also that not every lyric has to rhyme. If a lyric you're writing feels right with few or no rhymes, let it grow that way. Rhyme is a choice, not a must; it is one of many musical word games we can play to enliven our lyrics. "Chattanooga choo choo, woncha choo choo me home"—is that rhyme, alliteration, elision, or some nutty combination of all three? Whatever it is, it works.

Any words in any combination can make a good lyric, from the silk-and-martini words of Manhattan songwriters to the harsh four-letter words of Bronx rappers. Most words in lyrics are short and informal: "You don't know the one who dreams of you at night." We could call long formal words like "maturation," "certitude," or "recoupment" nonlyric-like, except that

Frank Loesser stuffed a textbook full of scientific polysyllables into "Adelaide's Lament":

> The average unmarried female,
> Basically insecure,
> Due to some long frustration may react
> With psychosomatic symptoms
> Difficult to endure
> Affecting the upper respiratory tract.

Lyrics don't have to be grammatically correct, they don't have to make sense (I still don't what "I Am the Walrus" means), and they can happily blither into wordless absurdity like the nonsense syllables of the 1950s hit, "The Witch Doctor": "Oo-ee-oo-ah-ah, ting-tang-walla-walla-bing bang / Oo-ee-oo-ah-ah, ting-tang-walla-walla-bing bang!"

Only one rule governs lyric writing: Lyrics must say something. The words of a song are not the means for mumbling shapeless ideas under your breath like, "Well … um … you see, before I went … you know, I mean, um …." Lyrics are a means of speaking up loudly and clearly on subjects you care about. Say what you please in your lyric, but say it with confidence. Even that silly "Oo-ee-oo-ah-ah" is not random babbling. Sing one "oo-ee" out of place and you'll realize what a strong statement the nonsense makes.

This rock-bottom demand that a lyric say something has given me one tried-and-true method for getting past writing roadblocks. Like every artist, I have dozens of tricks to tease my muse out of hiding. I sit down at my desk and my mind goes blank, so I straighten up my papers, tune my guitar, pace around the room, or run downstairs to check the mail. I sit down again, scribble something, cross it out, scribble again, then dash to the kitchen to refill my coffee cup. If I do that every day, with inspiration and perspiration blended in the traditional one to ninety-nine percent formula, the finished product slowly adds up. But on those days when I am well and truly stuck, I drop my pen, take off my guitar, stand up, look at the wall or out the window, and say aloud: "What do I want to say?"

When that doesn't work, I say louder and with more emphasis, "What do I really want to say? What do I want to say *right now*?"

More times than I can count, demanding an immediate answer to "What do I want to say?" has brought a grouping of words floating up from the depths to the surface of my mind, words that, in a baldly direct way, get across the heart of what I hope to convey. They are not words I've chosen for artful reasons. Often I am road-blocked because I've become too artful. Instead, these are words risen to answer an imperative, penetrating question. These words I treasure and write down with care. Even if they sound stupid or pretentious, I do not cross them out or change them right away. Whether in the end I use them intact, rewrite them ten times, or throw them out altogether, doesn't matter; they have given me a new starting point, connected me to my lyric's central purpose.

We may divide what lyrics convey into two practical if not precise categories, *feelings* and *ideas.*

Of the two, feelings come first. All lyrics convey colors from the age-old spectrum of human emotion: love, hate, joy, fear, rage, regret, pride, hope, envy, faith, yearning, and sorrow. Lyricists struggle to find those few words that will convey the finest shades of feeling to other people. This is no easy task. Feelings, as we all know, are slippery little devils always hiding under new masks, wriggling out of our grasp when we try to pin them down. Though evanescent, feelings have enormous power. Hungers of the spirit drive us onward as urgently as do hungers of the body. Storms of feeling can mark entire lives for good or for ill. Love gone wrong can break a human heart. For a lucky few, "Love is lovelier the second time around."

To write feelings into your lyrics, you must observe emotions in yourself and in other people, and you must admit the truth of what you observe. Pretend feelings, made-up-to-please feelings, imitated feelings will not cut the mustard. To write a good lyric you have to, as one great lyric puts it, "get down to the real nitty-gritty." This does not mean you need be blatant or cynical. Modesty and innocence have their own nitty-gritty, so do silliness and romance. It means, as always, tell the truth.

Your own emotions will always be the greatest font of feelings for your lyrics. An event may stir you so deeply one day that, while still frenzied, you'll search for words to express all you are feeling. Out of your pain or joy may come a strong clear statement: "Hold me tight, I'm scared tonight," or "Leave me, leave me alone," or "This is the worst worst day of my life." From that primal scream a lyric may grow. More often, time will give you the perspective to write about major upheavals. The best poems, Wordsworth famously said, convey "emotion recollected in tranquility." Writing lyrics directly from your own feelings can be harrowing, but stay honest to their twists and turns even when they expose embarrassing weakness, you'll mine pure gold. People love honest, emotional songs as generous gifts that help them untangle their own mixed feelings. Be honest too about your strengths. Think of the unconquerable passion of "I Will Survive," the head-over-heels exuberance of "I'm Singin' in the Rain," lyrics that equal in fervor soul-baring ballads like "Going Down Slow" and "Good Morning, Heartache."

The ups and downs of your friends and neighbors will open a second gold-mine for your lyrics. "Thank God for other people," a wise rabbi once said, and ain't it the truth. Imagine living alone like Robinson Crusoe on his island, with no other soul to talk to and listen to, and worst of all, no third soul for you and the second soul to gossip about. Except for a few hermits, humans crave company. We need nearly constant contact with others to feel content, to feel like ourselves, and we gladly put up with the myriad rubs of social life to share its more myriad joys. Observing other people's emotions—a teenaged boy and girl mooning along the street hand in hand, a little boy bawling over a dropped ice cream cone, a married couple screaming mad about money—may be pleasant or scary but will raise the curtain on the never-ending drama of human life. The more deeply you can see into the Joe and Jane comedies and tragedies playing all around you, the more your lyrics will convey feelings that Joe and Jane will recognize as true.

Whatever emotions you observe in other people, I guarantee you that they will remind you of your own. They may be different in detail, but they will be alike in essence. You live in your unique emotional world, I in mine, and other people in theirs, yet, with generous allowance made for exception and variation, what we love and hate, others love and hate. What scares us, scares them. What elates us, elates them. What pains us, pains them too. We lyricists can, therefore, trust to the emotional bond that ties us to people of all walks of life around the world:

> As I feel, you feel;
> As you feel, I feel.

Find yourself in others and others in yourself, and your listeners will hear your lyrics as sympathetic expressions of what they know in their hearts.

An obvious note, but still worth making, is that you do not have to experience every feeling you write as intensely as you paint it in your lyric, good news if you're writing a song about a murderer. *Imagination* is another must of lyric writing, the wonderful ability we have to dream up new worlds and people, to describe them as if they were real. Imagination's springboard word is *if,* two letters that build all the castles in Spain. Anytime is a good time for getting the stimulating bounce of a good "if." What if I were a cowboy, Mata Hari, an egg, the President? What if I lived in Rome in 3 A.D. or on Mars in 3003 A.D.? While wandering through your daydreams, notice how imagination needs some scrap of reality to feed on. We construct make-believe worlds by connecting and transforming elements we know from the real world. An imaginative lyricist like Sheb Wooley can create a purple people-eater only because we already know what purple, people, and eating are, and under the song's cheerful influence, we enjoy combining them in this silly way.

As Sheb Wooley mix-matched his way into his purple people-eater, we can mix–match emotions we have felt to imagine emotions we haven't felt. Let's say you are a happily married woman who wants to write a lyric about a shattering romantic breakup. You might think something like, "Well, I've had my share of heartache. After breaking up with Fred senior year, I cried my way through many sleepless nights. Okay, I got over Fred and met my true love Bob. But what if I hadn't met Bob and had become obsessed with Fred? God, remember how I became obsessed with my dolly in kindergarten? That was intense. What if I had started drinking to forget Fred? I've been drunk a few times. What if I were drunk all the time?" Keep asking yourself "what if?" questions like that and, just as with the "What do I want to say?" question, images, words, and phrases will rise in your mind to convey, truthfully, the colors and tastes of feelings, which, as raw experience, may be beyond your ken.

Short, commonly used words convey feelings best. Emotion speaks, not in big words like "schadenfreude," but in little words that everybody knows like, "I'm glad you're sad." Set up an emotion verb in a simile—"I love you like . . ." "I miss you like . . ."—then complete the simile with a vivid image—"like a hound dog loves his bone," "like an old sailor misses the sea." Listen for common sayings that everybody uses because they express emotions everybody feels. Lyrics like "Don't Blame Me," "Come Rain or Come Shine," and "I'm Sitting on Top of the World" have used up a few such sayings, but millions more keep popping up in everyday speech. A lyricist's greatest triumph may be to invent a phrase so expressive of a common feeling that it becomes a popular saying. Since I love lyrics, I know that Sammy Cahn wrote "Call Me Irresponsible," Johnny Mercer wrote "Something's Gotta Give," and Ira Gershwin wrote "Let's Call the Whole Thing Off," but I'd bet that many people who use the expressions have no idea which came first, the song or the saying.

Ideas form the lesser half of what lyrics convey. "I want, I need, I love" feelings are more at home in poetry, and "I believe, I argue, I declare" ideas are more at home in prose. Yet poetry can express ideas with striking force, and we can write lyrics to convey what we think as well as what we feel.

What do I mean by ideas as distinct from feelings? To put it simply: Ideas sum up feelings. I could, for example, convey the core feeling of an "I miss you" lyric with several emotion-filled phrases: "I'm so lonely tonight," "I wish you were in my arms," "Why did you leave me crying?" Then I could draw a conclusion from the feelings: "It's hard to get used to livin' alone," "Love ain't all easy street," "Broken hearts can't be mended."

Those phrases convey ideas. Yes, they support the core emotion, but they are more than pure feeling; they make general statements, and they attempt to define truths of human life. Many fine lyrics communicate profound ideas that ring true year after year like, "Time waits for no one," or "Everybody plays the fool sometime." Other lyrics convey sprightly ideas that connect more sporadically to eternal verity. Is life "just a bowl of cherries?" Sometimes yes, sometimes no. Is it true that "Love sucks?" We won't find the answer in a laboratory, but on those blue days when we feel love sucks, love sucks.

Ask yourself questions to bring up ideas in your mind: What do I believe? What have I learned from living? What is my philosophy? Why do I agree with one public speaker and disagree with another? If you form ideas that you earnestly want to share with other people, speak up. The healthy life of families, businesses, towns, and whole nations depend on everybody chipping in with their best ideas about how to work out problems and improve everyone's lot. As a lyricist you have a powerful way to contribute to the ongoing debates of your time.

Write your ideas in short, common words. Big ideas don't need big words, certainly not in lyrics—Lennon and McCartney convey an enormous idea in five syllables, "All you need is love." Don't be too strident with your ideas. Remember, as Johnny Mercer wrote, "How little we know." If your words get too heavy with ideas, you're writing a lecture, not a lyric. Keep feelings foremost, but again I urge you to not be shy about putting your beliefs into your lyrics. People are always looking for ideas to guide them, to help them understand day-to-day mysteries. When good ideas come, not laboring in dull newspaper prose, but lifted by melody's lilt and the pulse of rhythm, they can reach listeners with unforgettable force. John Lennon's "Imagine" or Bob Dylan's "The Times They Are A-Changing" are two of many idea-lyrics that have helped countless people "accentuate the positive" in their lives.

chapter 6

Song Forms

Beyond the chord structures that we've taken a first look at, songs have *forms*, larger structures that determine the shape and length of those chord structures.

Songs come in an endless number of forms. A look over the long history of songs would unearth many oddities, and, who knows, you may invent one yourself. Yet as practical fact, a half-dozen song forms include ninety percent of the popular songs written in the past century, and I predict that the same forms or close derivatives will still dominate popular songs a century hence. Here are the half-dozen:

1. The Eight-Bar Folk Song: AA

The *eight-bar folk song* is the simplest common song form. It consists of eight measures of three–four or four–four time, usually with a tonic-dominant chord structure and a short, repetitive melody and lyric. At the end of *Chord Structure—Part I* are eight-bar songs, and so is "He's Got the Whole World in His Hands":

Example 41 Track Three

This form, called AA (though it could be called AAAAA . . .), is one that you must pound into your head by any and all means necessary. Play and sing "He's Got the Whole World," "Michael, Row the Boat Ashore," and "Rock-a-My Soul," until the swing of those eight bars going round and round work their way deep into your hands, your voice, and your soul. On manuscript paper, set up eight blank bars:

Example 42

Then experiment with putting I, IV, and V chords in different bars. You'll soon see that forms that begin and end on the I chord feel the most stable. You start at home, you go somewhere, and you come back home:

Example 43 Track Three

If you end the form on a V chord, you'll feel a certain suspense—the V chord acts like a comma—that readies you to turn smoothly around to begin the form again:

Example 44 Track Three

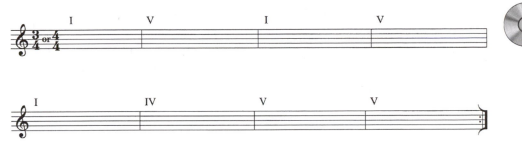

The last time round, of course, you'll play a ninth measure and end on a final I chord—the period—to bring you to rest at home.

As you begin to get a feel for the eight-bar form, you'll see how it's often divided into two and four-bar units. The next example is a little song of mine with phrases that rhyme every two bars. The first two phrases create a four-bar front half, and the second two create a four-bar back half. Note how naturally the lyrics and melody follow the form, creating an easy sing–breathe, sing–breathe rhythm:

Example 45 Track Three

The eight-bar AA form is important because thousands of wonderful songs are eight bars long, and because those eight bars are the building blocks of many more complex songs and musical forms. Many long passages of chamber and symphonic music are constructed in eight-bar units. Getting the eight-bar form in your bones will open many doors and answer many questions.

What is the only problem with round-and-round eight-bar songs? They get boring. After a dozen or so *A*s, singer and listener may long for a new section to contrast with the first. Hence, the second most common form.

2. The Sixteen-Bar Verse-Chorus Form: AB

The *sixteen-bar verse–chorus* structure, known as AB, doubles the eight-bar form. "My Darling Clementine" is a classic sixteen-bar AB. The eight-bar verses tell the story ("In a cabin, in a canyon....") with new lyrics for every verse, and the eight-bar chorus repeats one lyric for the sing-a-long refrain ("Oh, my darling, oh my darling ..."):

Example 46 Track Three

Note that the only difference between "Clementine's" A and B lies in the lyrics; the chord structure and melody of each are identical. Yet such is our delight in the verse–chorus alternation that the two eight-bar sections give us all the contrast we need. In "Oh, Susanna," another great verse–chorus song, the chorus has its own melody. To follow the lyric, we sing two verses before going on to the chorus, so the form of "Oh, Susanna'" is really a twenty-four-bar AAB:

Example 47 Track Three

OH, SUSANNA

Stephen Foster

VERSE

I come from Al - a - bam - a with my ban - jo on my knee, I'm
It rained all night the day I left, The weath-er it was dry, The

goin' to Lou - si - a - na there my true love for to see.
sun so hot I froze to death, Su - san - na, don't you cry.

CHORUS

Oh, Su - san - na, oh don't you cry for me, For I

come from Al - a - bam - a with my ban - jo on my knee.

Verse–chorus songs are perennial pop favorites, and they work, as "Oh, Susanna" does, when the verse sets up the chorus so perfectly that listeners can't help joining in. Dolly Parton's hit, "Nine to Five," is a fine example of the form. We're quiet as Dolly tells a personal story in the verse, then, finding our story in hers, we happily jump in on the universal chorus—"Working nine to five …".

3. The Thirty-Two-Bar Standard Form: AABA

"Ain't Misbehavin'," "Stormy Weather," and "Your Cheating Heart" are three of countless American pop songs that take the *thirty-two-bar standard form*. This common but challenging form divides its thirty-two bars into four eight-bar sections: an opening A section followed by a second A, then a contrasting B section or bridge, and back to a final A (AABA). So many songs fit the thirty-two-bar AABA form that some call it "pop's cookie cutter," but I love AABA. It's long enough but not too long, clear but subtle, and though grown from a burnished tradition, still fresh with poetic possibilities. Make it one of your goals, as it is mine, to write a thirty-two-bar classic like "I Got Rhythm," "Body and Soul," or "Blue Moon."

Here is a no-frills, thirty-two-bar chord structure to represent the form:

Example 48 Track Three

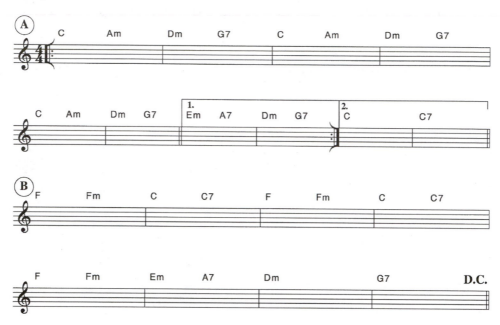

Crucial to the AABA form is that the B section must contrast with the A section. B must differ enough from A for listeners to hear it and know, even if they don't know why, "Ah, one part of the song repeats a lot, the other part comes along less often." The melody, harmony, rhythm, and lyrics of the B section all contribute to creating the contrast. B section lyrics, for example, can come from a new point of view. The singer sees the bright side of life in the A section and admits the dark side in the bridge. One way most, if not all, AABA songs heighten the A-B contrast is by *modulating*, changing to a new key in the bridge. Modulation sounds scary, but be brave. Look at the song above, play it, and review all you know about chords and keys.

See all those C–A minor-D minor-G7 chords going around every two bars in the A sections? They show we're in the key of C. The first time we play the A, we end on a G7, the V chord, turning us around to the I chord at the top of the second A. But the second A needs a new ending because it's going on to the bridge, so it ends on a C7. C7, remember, is the V of F, the IV chord. Sure enough, the bridge starts on an F chord and has F and F minor chords throughout, until the last four bars when the chords wend their way back to a full bar of G7, which leads us to the C at the top of the third A.

What's happened? We've modulated from the key of C into the key of F for the bridge, then modulated back to C as the last A approached. Bridges can and do modulate to many contrasting keys, but this I to IV modulation is among the most common. (See it above in "Oh, Susanna.") A glance at the Circle of Fifths shows why. C and F are closely related keys. Modulating between them creates an A–B contrast distinct enough to be effective, but also a smoother, closer contrast than, let's say, a long jagged leap to G# minor.

4. Twelve-Bar Blues

With the *twelve-bar blues* we leave the European tradition of eight-bars combined in ever larger forms and enter a new tradition, a musical tradition with African roots, born in America a century ago. Far more than a musical form, the blues are the heart and soul of African–American music, the cornerstone of jazz, rock 'n' roll, and much pop and country music. Beloved today around the world, the blues play over wide spectrums of color, rhythm, and emotion. They convey a wisdom that takes a long lifetime to imbibe.

Yet in a mysterious way, the blues are their form. Play the basic chords to a steady four–four beat through the twelve bars, sing the lyrics with feeling, and you are launched as a blues singer. With time and hard work, you will improve. Here is a simple blues to represent the form:

Example 49 Track Three

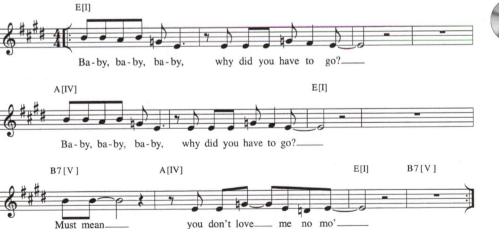

Note that the twelve bars are divided into three groups of four bars. Here, as often but not always occurs, the first two groups repeat the same lyric while the third concludes with a rhyming line. Note too that the melody doesn't fill the form; there's plenty of space after the end of "why did you have to go?" for another voice or instrument to respond to the singer:

Example 50

why did you have to   go?____ (Why did you have   to,   why did you have   to)

Note how firmly the blues form is built on its nearly invariable I–IV–V chord structure. Let's put the twelve bars in a straight line:

Example 51

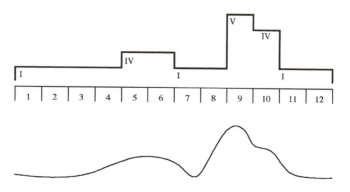

Now we can see clearly the musical curve that give the blues its dramatic power. Each form (or chorus, in common parlance) starts on the tonic as ground, climbs to the subdominant, falls back to the tonic, climbs still higher to a brief peak on the dominant, then tumbles again to earth. The more you feel the blues forms rise and fall, its eternal drama of struggle and acceptance, the more the blues you write and sing and play will add authentically to the glorious tradition of the blues.

The blues offers two great advantages to the songwriter. First, audiences love the blues; any pop performer will tell you to keep a few blues in your bag as sure-fire people-pleasers. Second, the blues are infinitely adaptable. Despite their standard form and chord structure, the blues can take on any musical mood from deathly despair to head-over-heels happiness. Chuck Berry, Bob Dylan, and Marvin Gaye have written blues in such different styles that it is hard to believe that "Johnny B. Goode," "Leopard-Skin Pillbox Hat," and "Wonderful One," are all built on the same form. But listen again. In all three you'll hear the old blues rise and fall that goes back through Muddy Waters to Bessie Smith and before.

5. The Double Sixteen-Bar Form

All the forms described above have variants, but the *double sixteen-bar form* seems sometimes to be all variants. Many songs fit the form but in subtly different ways. In essence, the double sixteen-bar form is a long form. The first sixteen bars make one extended section The second sixteen start out like the first, but, at about the midpoint, they go in a new direction that brings the whole thirty-two bars to a close. The big band ballad "Out of Nowhere" represents the form well. See how we start the song and go ahead without any repeats for sixteen measures, then loop back to the top, but after ten measures turn to a new ending:

Example 52 Track Three

The best way to get a feel for the fluid double-sixteen form is to study great songs in the form—"Goody Goody," "Bye, Bye Blackbird," "Fly Me to the Moon"—and finding, underneath the variations, their common loose, long-limbed quality. Instead of circling back all the time as AABAs do, double-sixteens keep charging ahead. That's why jazzmen love to improvise on them, and that's why they suit optimistic, exuberant lyrics like, "When you're smiling, the whole world smiles with you."

6. The Endless Boogie

The newest common song form is the *endless boogie*, one chord played to a danceable rhythm pattern as long as a performer wants to play it. Like the blues, the endless boogie has African roots; John Lee Hooker and Bo Diddley introduced one-chord grooves to American pop music in the 1950s, and James Brown and the hip-hop generation have kept them high in the charts ever since. The danger of the form is boredom, but when powered by seductive beats, endless boogies become dynamos of musical energy that can shake stadiums and get thousands of people chanting the same funky lyrics: "You're gonna give your love to me, you're gonna give your love to me...".

Endless boogies are not shapeless boogies. "Bo Diddley," the 1955 hit that set the form, is built from two-bar lyric phrases and two-bar instrumental answer phrases, making four-bar units. Each four-bar unit has its own four answering unit, and since four and four make eight, with the endless boogie form, we've found our way back to our eight-bar folk song, AAAAAAA:

Example 53 Track Three

Bo Didd-ley, Bo Didd-ley,   where you been?

Been down-town   and   back a - gain!___

These six are not the only song forms. Some songs have C and D sections, which are quirky two- or four-bar added units that break up the endless repeats of As and Bs. Sometimes an A turns out to need ten measures, and many blues are eight and sixteen bars long. One song of mine, "Such a Tender Touch," has an eight-bar A section and a ten-bar B section and rolls around ABAB. This creates an oddball eighteen-bar form I've never used before and may never use again. That oddball, however, grew naturally out of the music and lyrics, and your oddballs will occur likewise. You'll write an absolutely standard AB verse–chorus song about Tommy the Tuba and find you need a silly four bars—"Tommy sang toot, tootie-toot-toot-toot"—to stick in here and there for comic effect.

As you try your hand at these six forms and your own inventions, remember one simple rule: except for the blues, *nearly all songs are built from eight-bar sections*. Look for those eight-bar sections as you write, feel for them as you play, and you'll surely find the plain framework that supports the most complex compositions.

chapter 7
Melody

"A pretty girl is like a melody," says a wonderful lyric. Turn the sentiment around and it's still true: a melody is like a pretty girl, capricious and captivating. Like moonlight sparkling on rippled water or colts frolicking in a field, melodies come to our ears as gifts of natural beauty: the merry plash of a brook, pine trees sighing in the wind, a whippoorwill calling mournfully into the summer dusk. Melodies also come as gifts of human innocence: the lullabies your mother sang you in the crib, the ballad that became "our song" for you and your mate, a folk tune from your native land that always brings a tear to your eye. In this mean old world, we may well thank God for melody. How many times, when stooped by work or worry, have we heard a lively air riding a breeze along the street and through an open window, a catchy few notes that get us humming? Soon, without our willing it, a smile tugs on our lips and new hope surges in our hearts.

More properly defined, a melody is the sound of one voice making music: a cricket, a frog, a robin, a drum, a baby cooing, an old woman laughing, or Louis Armstrong playing his bold and tender trumpet. Whatever the tune or the setting, melody is the song of one soul crying in the wilderness, whistling in the dark, calling out, "Hello out there, this is me, who are you?" For us songwriters, melody is everything. We are at bottom solo singers. Even when a maestro merges many melodies into a symphony with grand overarching harmonies, we can still hear the melody of each instrument: the bass viol's round tones bouncing gravely along (tum-ti-tum), the cello, the viola, and the violin melodies darting and surging in counterpoint above, the trumpets and trombones having their brassy say, and deep in this musical forest, an oboe and a flute entwining their melodies like fauns dancing in a sun-dappled meadow.

Melody calls to the universe with music as its medium. From the twelve tones and the tones between them, from smooth scales and staggered arpeggios, from the beats of rhythm and the shades of timbre, melody spins its long looping lines of sound, graceful as rose boughs on a trellis, each note a blossom. These lines may seem delicate, here for a moment, gone forever, but don't be deceived. Melodic lines are as tough as a spider's thread, able to bear all the emotion and experience we can pour into them. Melody is a most effective, and most sensitive, way to talk to other people and be understood.

What makes melody beautiful? Why does one melody soar and another fall flat? These are unanswerable questions. Melody's ways and powers are far too mysterious to obey hard and fast rules—"This will make a beautiful melody, that will make a dull one." So instead of approaching the beauty of melody head on, let's come at the subject from the side and ask, "What is the goal of melody? What do we want melody to do?" By focusing on melody's usefulness, we may come across its beauty unawares.

The great goal of melody is to create a line of musical sound so vivid and enjoyable that other people will want to sing it themselves in their own way. From this springs my only rule for writing melody: Try to make your melodies contagious. You won't always succeed, of course, but keep trying to write melodies that other people will want to sing. Singability, that's what you're after, melodies with so natural a grace and symmetry that they're readily understood, gladly sung, and long remembered.

How do we construct such melodies? Seldom, fortunately, from the absolute scratch of, "Let's see, I'll start on a quarter note G and then, hmmm, go on to an eighth note B and eighth note D." We trust, instead, that an inspired spark will kick-start the melody writing process. One day as I'm warming up on my guitar, a phrase, a few notes in a rhythm, pop into my head, maybe a few words attached. At first, I'm not thinking G, B, D and eighth notes at all, just, "La-di-da, girl, you look lovely tonight." If, as I keep strumming and singing, the phrase keeps intriguing me and, better yet, leads me to a second good phrase, then I think, "Maybe I've got a song here." I grab my favorite pencil and a sheet of manuscript paper, and in my first henscratching, I find out that my "La-di-da" looks like this:

Example 54

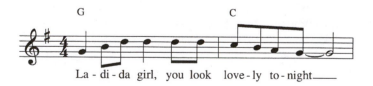

La - di - da girl, you look love-ly to-night____

From there on come a few hours or days of headscratching, howling this note and that note, putting down the guitar, picking up the guitar and writing with it over my knee. My big questions are: Where is this melody going? How is it going to get there? How I can I get it back home again? Sometimes the melody tells me where it's going—that F to B natural jump is in there, like it or nor—but often I spend hours debating various directions the line could take. My goal, always, is singability, and I choose this note or that, this rhythm or that, because I find it trips more easily off the tongue and falls more pleasingly on the ear. The process is, at most, half rational, but I do try, consciously, to build into my melodies these people-pleasing qualities: *curve*, *lilt*, *logical link to the chords*, *tonal and rhythm patterns*, and *climax-resolution*.

To see how to build a melody with these qualities, let's set up an eight-bar song form with a simple and familiar chord structure. On it we'll write an extremely simple melody, whole notes on the root tones of chords:

Example 55 Track Four

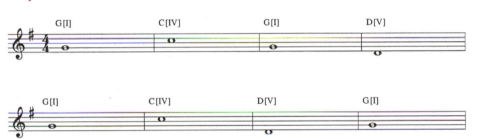

Written an octave or two lower, that melody might make a fine bass line, and it is logically linked to its chords. Yet I can't imagine anybody leaving a show humming this slow whole note melody or singing an eight-syllable lyric that might fit it, such as, "I … love … you … so … / Oh … please … don't … go." How can we rewrite this melody to give it the qualities we are looking for? First, we can turn those whole-note straight lines into curves. Here's a new quarter-note melody for the first two measures:

Example 56 Track Four

That melody moves in short steps along the G major scale, going note-to-note except for the final small jump from E to G. Melodies most often move like this, stepwise along the scale of the key being played, but lilt requires us to leap up sometimes from a low to a high note, skipping five, six, or even an octave of steps. Here are the same two measures:

Example 57 Track Four

Both of these melodies demonstrate a logical link between melody and chords. Most of the tones in both melodies are "safe notes" that are in the triads being played in each measure. The few non-chord tones are unaccented *passing tones* that connect chord tones. Lovely melodies may be written using only chord tones played as *arpeggios*, the tones coming one after another instead of being sounded all at once:

Example 58 Track Four

Yet if we always play it safe, we risk dullness. How can we give the link between melody and chords a captivating twist? One way is to start not, as we've done so far, at the safest place, *do*, the root of the tonic chord, but to move the melody's opening note to *mi* or *sol*, still in the chord but a bit off-center:

Example 59 Track Four

Another way is to emphasize a melody tone that belongs to two chords in succession. The same G will sound different in the first and second measures because in the first it's the root of the I triad and in the second it's the top of the IV triad:

Example 60 Track Four

We can further twist chord–melody logic by bringing tones not in the triads to prominent points of the melody, instead of half-hiding them as passing tones. In *Chord Structures—Part II* we'll delve deeper into expanded chords, but let it suffice here to say that to any 1–3–5 triad may be added other tones, which multiply its chordal colors. For example, adding an A to the top of a C major triad makes a C major 6th chord (1–3–5–6) and adding a B makes a C major 7th chord (1–3–5–7):

Example 61

Play them both, and listen to the shimmer of mystery the new tones bring to the all-too-logical triads. Construct your melodies around non-triad tones like these, and you'll open up many challenging emotional and musical possibilities:

Example 62 Track Four

So far we've used only tones on the G major scale. Now we can introduce notes off the scale for flashes of discordant color:

Example 63

All these melody fragments have tonal and rhythmic patterns, but we can make such patterns prominent in a melody, often together. The tonal pattern of these major thirds, bouncing between the first and third steps of each chord, doubles the rhythm pattern of the repeated eighth notes:

Example 64 Track Four

A melody can emphasize tonal patterns by making one tone a steady point and varying the interval it bounces across to a new tone. Composer Ellen Mandel wrote a lovely melody for a poem by E.E. Cummings that uses this device strikingly. Hear how the first note of each measure moves down a half-step while the other notes stay the same:

Example 65

Rhythm patterns are so vital to melody that even a one-note melody can be interesting if it's set to a catchy beat. Listen to the offbeat rhythm pattern kept by the claves in Latin music:

Example 66 Track Four

Melodic phrases that suit lyrics and the human voice include long tones for important words and rests for breath:

Example 67 Track Four

We need all these elements—curve, lilt, logical link to the chords, tonal and rhythm patterns—to construct a melody line that rises to a climax and then ebbs away to resolution, and we need to let the melody wend its way through the whole eight bars. Here's an eight-bar melody I just wrote, no work of genius to be sure, but one that demonstrates the qualities we've been looking at:

Example 68 Track Four

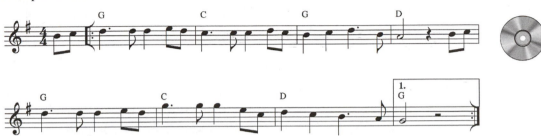

Note that the melody starts with two notes before the form's first downbeat. That's a *pickup*, a common device that gets us off to a lilting start. The first two bars have a ♩. ♪♩ ♫ rhythm pattern that I vary slightly in the third. The fourth bar ends the opening phrase with a held note and a rest for breath. The second phrase opens with the same tones and rhythm pattern as the first but then leaps to a high G, our climax, from which we tumble back down the octave to end on the tonic G.

If we want to expand that eight-bar A section into an AABA song, we need to write a bridge with its own melody. Our bridge, as we saw in *Song Forms*, must contrast with the A section, and we can contribute to that contrast by giving the B section melody markedly different tonal and rhythm patterns:

Example 69 Track Four

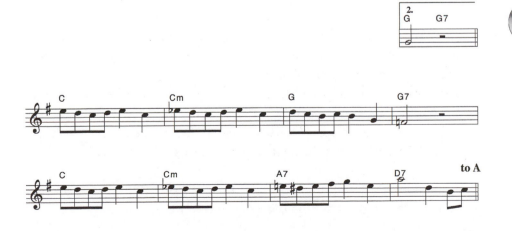

But note that this B section, like its A, is shaped into two four-bar phrases with a held-note pause in the fourth bar to divide them, and that it builds to its own climax before jumping down to use the opening pickup to get us back to A again.

Experiment with these and similar musical devices, pray for inspiration, study melodies you already love, keep in shape with daily practice, and you will in time learn to write curving, lilting melodies that link logically with their chords, have catchy tonal and rhythm patterns, and build to exciting climaxes—melodies, in a word, that people love to sing.

Here are five tips:

- Don't get too rangy. Keep your melody within an octave and a half, and better yet, a ninth or tenth from lowest to highest note. You want a melody with a range that anyone who likes to sing can sing.

    As a footnote to that, don't let your melody stay high for too long. Singability depends as much on *tessitura*, where most of the melody lies, as it does on range. Experienced singers know that handling a few high peaks is much easier than scraping their vocal ceiling measure after measure.
- Do not strain for effects. Look for interesting leaps and landing places, but keep your melodies easy and natural. Your goal is not to awe your audience with your genius, but to get them singing with you as friends.
- Rewrite. Just because you scratched a melody down one way doesn't mean it's cast in stone. As you sing a new song, listen for dull patches and awkward turns, and do what you need to do to fix them.
- Don't become too attached to every note of your melodies. Legends say that the liberties jazz singer Billie Holiday took with their sacred melodies appalled Cole Porter and Richard Rodgers. Well, too bad for them. Pop song melodies are not and will never be as fixed as classical melodies. When someone else sings our songs, chances are they'll adapt the melodies in big and small ways to suit their voices. If we're smart, we'll let them. Why? Because we do the same thing. Six months of singing a melody always changes—and improves—what I wrote down at first.
- Let a song go out of your heart. Melody springs from the primal urge to lift our voices and express feelings overflowing in our souls. Trust your own voice, your own choices. Don't let yourself get tangled up in technique. Melody *is* like a pretty girl, enticing and elusive. Don't fence her in.

Let's conclude by playing and singing "Danny Boy." A Harvard professor declared in the 1920s that this old Irish fiddle tune, first known as "The

Londonderry Air," stands among the most beautiful melodies in music, and according to my mother who attended his lectures, the professor analyzed in detail how well the melody blends all the qualities of curve and lilt, pattern and climax, that we're looking for. I too find "Danny Boy" beautiful—I'm Irish–American and tear up every time I hear it—but beauty is ever a matter of opinion. If we ask, however, does "Danny Boy" reach the goal of melody? Does it have what a melody needs to be loved and sung by millions? Is "Danny Boy" singable? To these questions, passing centuries of singers will always answer yes.

Example 70 Track Four

DANNY BOY
(Londonderry Air)

chapter 8

Rhythm

Rhythm, the equal of melody and harmony in music's holy trinity, is of utmost importance to pop music. There's no higher praise for a pop song than "It's got a beat you can dance to." It's worth noting that pop music rhythm embodies two major innovations in Western music history. Given all we have to cover in this book, however, we must skim past its many and fascinating intricacies and dwell only on a few facts that underlie nearly all American pop song rhythms for the past one hundred years.

First, with only a handful of exceptions, pop songs come in one of two meters, 3/4 time:

Example 71

or 4/4 time:

Example 72

Of the two, 4/4 time is far more common. Listening to pop songs on the radio, you can nearly always count along "**1** 2 3 4 **1** 2 3 4." Every once in a while you'll need to count along "**1** 2 3 **1** 2 3."

Let's deal briefly with 3/4 time. Pop songs in 3/4 time are most often played in a *waltz* feel, with a strong accent on the first beat, the classic OOM-pah-

pah of "The Blue Danube Waltz," "Anniversary Waltz," and many other romantic evergreens. Listen to my "Valentine Waltz":

Example 73 Track Five

Jazz songwriters (and players and singers) love jazz waltzes that offset OOM-pah-pah into something lighter and more swinging, for instance:

Example 74 Track Four

Doubling up 3/4 into 6/8 can be a good way to give a song a lilting Italian quality:

Example 75

That's about it for 3/4, here at least. Songs in waltz time are a sometime thing for me, happening less by plan than by an accident of the melody, lyric, or mood that gets me started. Do try writing a waltz or two to get the feeling of its cushioned bounce. Who knows? You might write a hit as big as "The Tennessee Waltz."

4/4 time is so common that musicians often call it just that, *common time*, and indicate the meter with a big C at the start of a song:

Example 76

4/4 time, as played in American pop songs, embodies two major innovations: *steady tempo*—the music's pace does not change from the start to the end of a song—and the *backbeat*—the accented beats of each measure fall on 2 and 4:

Example 77 Track Five

Dances and marches had long been played in Europe and America at a steady 4/4 tempo, sometimes accented on 2 and 4, but most classical music makes 1 and 3 the dominant *downbeats* of each measure and 2 and 4 the weaker *upbeats*. The musicians play in *fluid tempo*, speeding the music up or slowing it down to suit the mood, as a soprano may do, for instance, holding a big note while the conductor keeps the orchestra simmering beneath her. Not until African musical ideas began to spread in America with ragtime, jazz, and blues (about 1900) did steady tempo—"the groove," jazzmen call it—and the backbeat—"It's got a backbeat, you can't lose it," Chuck Berry sang about rock 'n' roll—become foundation concepts to which many musicians devote their lives.

Steady time and the backbeat became ever more popular in the 20th century, surviving every change in style. Duke Ellington snapped his fingers and Count Basie tapped his toes on the backbeat, Mahalia Jackson's gospel audiences clapped on the backbeat, and Hank Williams strummed his bluesy country songs on the backbeat. Jazz and pop music kept the 2–4 accent light and swinging until the 1950s when blues, R&B, and rock 'n' roll made it stomping and whomping: Elvis swung his pelvis on the backbeat. Steady time suited disco's drum machines and techno-pop's sequencers perfectly, and even in hip-hop's wacky beats I can hear a backbeat blended in the rhythm tracks.

This means that you need to learn to play at a steady tempo, to get into the groove of a song and stay there, and to play whatever shading of the backbeat, heavy or light, suits your taste and the song you're playing. Listen for the backbeat every time you turn on the radio or put on a pop CD. Clap with the crowd at a pop music concert. When you're playing, train yourself to tap your foot by lifting your toes on 1 and 3 and tapping on 2 and 4:

Example 78

Playing solo, you need to keep your offbeat clear. One way is to play a held bass note on 1 and 3 and a short treble chord on 2 and 4.

Example 79 Track Five

When playing in a band, you may not need to play so strong a boom-chick pattern because the drummer will most likely be laying down a boom-chick foundation by playing bass drum thumps on 1 and 3 and snare drum snaps on 2 and 4: whatever you play, you'll build on that foundation:

Example 80 Track Five

Snare Drum:

Bass Drum:

Pop songs do not give you Schubert and Schumann's luxury of writing "accelerando" or "ritandando" on your scores, directions to compress or stretch the song's tempo. You may play an introduction *rubato*, out of time, and you may *retard*, slow down, your endings, but most often you, and whoever else plays your songs, will count them off, "1, 2, 1 2 3 4," and stick to that tempo, allegro or largo, to the last note. The melodies you write will need to fit their phrases, pauses, and dramatic turns within steady-time's nonstop drive. Your lyrics likewise will need to flow in rhythmic accord with the backbeat pulse.

The secret of keeping steady time is to get physical. As you play, respond to the music's rhythm with your feet, legs, hips, butt, back, neck, head, shoulders, arms, and your hands. Move with the groove. The secret of making the backbeat second nature is to lay back. Or as a sax player whispered in my ear one night on the bandstand, "Get off of the 1, man." Backbeat musicians are not me-firsters who turn barlines into beachheads and plant "I am number 1!" flags at the start of every measure. Backbeat cats know, respect, and play 1, but they like to let 1 go by with an "After you, Alphonse," bow, and then speak their piece. The first two measures of George and Ira Gershwin's masterpiece, "Embraceable You" demonstrate perfectly the beauty and expressive value of the backbeat feeling:

Example 81

Em - brace me,   my sweet em–

George and Ira could have written:

Example 82

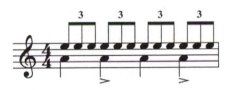

Em - brace me,   my sweet em–

but then "Embrace me" would sound like a lover insisting on his rights. George and Ira's "Embrace me" sounds like a caressing suggestion from a lover duly grateful for love.

Often but not always, a steady 4/4 backbeat comes with a further rhythmic development, eighth-note triplets played on each quarter-note of the measure:

Example 83 Track Five

Looks tricky, but give it a try and you'll soon catch the feeling. This is the rhythm the piano plays on The Platters' big hit, "The Great Pretender," and you can hear it on countless blues, jazz, rock, soul, and gospel songs. This "ching-ching-ching, ching-ching-ching" beat is called a *compound rhythm* because it combines a three-feeling with a four-feeling. You could call the rhythm 12/8 time because it does have twelve eighth notes in each measure, yet I find that the quarter notes march below predominant and think of it as 4/4 with a triplet feeling.

That triplet rhythm has given many a slow ballad rhythmic drive, but the rhythm matters even when kept as a background element in a song's rhythm. Why? Because the triplet feeling is the foundation of another vital element of pop song rhythm—*swing.*

Describing swing is a bit tricky, so pay attention. Play or clap this string of eighth notes:

Example 84 Track Five

They could be part of any melody you might write:

Example 85 Track Five

Ba-by, Ba-by, ba-by, don't you   know I love you so

But how are you going to play or sing them above the triplet feeling? Playing them as *straight eighth notes* that divide quarter notes in half will clash with the triplet's dividing the same quarter note into thirds. *Swing eighth notes* solve the problem by fattening the first eighth and slimming the second. The first eighth note gets the time value of the triplet's first two eighth notes, and the second gets the time value of the triplet's last eighth note:

Example 86

That way "Baby, baby, baby," doesn't come out an even "BA-BY BA-BY BA-BY," but a long-short "*BAA*-by *BAA*-by *BAA*-by" that fits perfectly with the triplet feeling underneath.

That's swing. Who can say why, but swing eighth notes over a 4/4 backbeat pulse can get people rocking and reeling. Swing had its heyday in the 30s and 40s when lindy hoppers danced to Benny Goodman, Count Basie, and Glenn Miller swinging pop songs. Too big to die with the big bands, swing found its way into much of rock 'n' roll and R&B and is still a surefire people-pleasing rhythm. Try swinging your own ballads and uptempo tunes. As Duke Ellington said, "It don't mean a thing, if it ain't got that swing."

Getting a feel for steady time, the backbeat, and swing opens the door on *syncopation*, and due again to its African roots, pop music is full of syncopation. Syncopation may be most simply defined as *accenting beats usually unaccented*. Pop music's primary syncopation is the backbeat, but that's only the beginning. Look at a Motown songbook and you'll see many big notes and chords landing, not on the downbeat 1 of a measure, but coming in early on the last eighth note of the bar before:

Example 87 Track Five

Look at a book of jazz songs, and you'll see similar "over the barline" syncopations as well as many melodic rhythm figures like these:

Example 88 Track Five

Compare how it feels to play those two examples with these nonsyncopated versions:

Example 89

and you'll sense the rubber ball bounce that syncopation can give your songs. Syncopated rhythms are trickier to play than long rows of dependable down-beats, but low rows of dependable downbeats can get dull. Let syncopation into your music. The fun makes the risk worthwhile, and there's nothing like syncopated upbeats to lift listeners' spirits and get them up out of their seats and dancing.

The Latin dance rhythms from the Caribbean and Brazil—still in steady 4/4 time—take syncopation to its height, blending the beats of many percussion instruments into *polyrhythms* that surge and flow in long complex patterns. The unifying thread for the *mambo*, *rhumba*, and many salsa rhythms is the *clave beat*, the unvarying rhythm kept by the claves, two round rosewood sticks clicked together like so, over and over again:

Example 90 Track Five

The clave rhythm, also found beneath the Bo Diddley and many rap and hip-hop beats, is so much the heart of Latin rhythm that when Brazilian claves players in the 1950s moved the second beat in the second measure one eighth-note later:

Example 91 Track Five

they set off a revolution called the *bossa nova*, the new beat.

Practice clapping, tapping, playing, and singing both the clave and bossa nova beat until you can keep both up without strain or mistake through numerous roll-arounds of a song. The new rhythms will give you new melodic and harmonic ideas—the bossa nova's soft sway always suggests to me feather-light melodies floating over pastel chords. Add a few salsas and bossas to the ballads and blues in your bag.

Two other pop song rhythms need brief mention: the *tango* and *reggae*. A sexy, dramatic dance from Argentina, the tango became wildly popular in the 1920s, making matinee idol Rudolph Valentino America's first Latin lover. That lurid history means that it's not easy to play a tango today without a hint of parody, yet as the music of the great Astor Piazzolla proves, the tango has rich expressive possibilities. No one beat like the clave beat underlies the tango, yet these two rhythms are key to the tango feel:

Example 92 Track Five

Reggae builds on the backbeat but backwards. Reggae drummers play their 2–4 accents on the bass drum, turning boom-chick into chicka-boom:

Example 93 Track Five

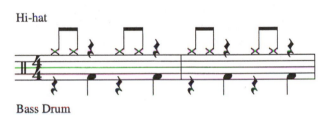

Americans who've been hearing boom-chick from birth may need disciplined study to get a good reggae feel. Without study, it's all too easy to hear those bass drum 2s and 4s as the backbeat's 1s and 3s and thus *turn the beat around*, as drummers say, reversing reggae's natural accent and getting out of the groove. Time studying and playing reggae will, however, be well spent. Only the reggae beat can create that ultra-laid back Jamaican sound that spread "One Love" around the world.

Experiment with these and other rhythms in your songwriting, but remember that most songwriters have one or two rhythms they are most comfortable with, beats bred in their bones. Chuck Berry wrote song after song with a hopped-up rock 'n' roll beat, Antonio Carlos Jobim penned dozens of softly lilting bossa novas, and Willie Nelson loves the lazy loping rhythms of Texas swing.

As you write and play, you'll find your home rhythm. Don't fight it. Somehow that rhythm belongs to you as part of your musical make-up, a gift from your native land, your ancestors, from God. Songs you write in your home rhythm may be your strongest.

Still, don't get stuck in one groove. Music has countless rhythms, and new rhythms are waiting to be discovered. Practice rhythms not born in your bones, and you'll learn to play them, if not like a native, well enough to write songs that use them. If your last two songs were blues rockers, tell yourself, "Today I'm going to try a Viennese waltz!" Take an old song and try it with a new rhythm. In my "Midnight in Manhattan," I wrote a swing rhythm to get a 30s New York jazz mood in the A sections and switched to a Latin feel for the bridge, hoping to capture today's vibrant streets at night:

> A Spanish bar, a flashy car,
> Two guys talking trash,
> A girl walks down from the corner,
> One guy hands the other cash.

People love all kinds of rhythms from country waltzes to Cuban rhumbas, but only if the beats are fresh, alert, and lively. Tired old grooves you fall into without thinking won't cut the mustard. To get your listeners up on their toes, stay on your toes yourself. In pop music, as the DJs say, the beat goes on.

chapter 9

Style and Story

So far we've looked at songs in their parts. Before re-looking at those parts in more detail, let's step back and look at songs as a whole, the sum of those many parts. You've finished a new song, and like the proud builder of a little log cabin, you put down your tools and take an inquiring walk around it, inside and out. As you sense its overall symmetries, ask yourself these two questions: "What style is this song in?" and "Does this song tell its story?"

Style

If you answer the style question, "It's the best song ever written; that's what style it is," then I understand. We musicians don't like our music labeled and put in boxes. "I don't play any kind of music," Louis Armstrong declared many times, "I play music." Duke Ellington described his music as "beyond category," often adding, "There are only two kinds of music: good music and bad music." Louis and Duke speak for us all. Yes, my personality, training, and heritage shape my music, but inside I'm acting on the same urge to play music that every musician acts on, no matter what sounds come out of us when we do. We are trying with our music to leap barriers, not erect them, and we're hoping for hits that will speak to anyone and everyone in the world.

Yet music does come in styles, not boxes exactly, but groupings that can be defined and within which many of us spend our creative lives. With Louis, I used to answer defiantly, "Music," when asked, "What kind of music do you play?" Now I answer more sensibly, "Easy-going pop-jazz," because those few words prepare listeners for what they're going to hear from me, where my style lies on music's broad spectrum of styles.

So what style is your song in? If you do not know or find it hard to say, now is the time to think the question through and come up with an answer. Yes, cling to the universal in your music, but also embrace the fact and value of song styles. We'll soon look at the commercial advantages of writing within song styles; here, let's look at the musical advantages.

Song styles may be defined by musical specifics: jazz songs swing their eighth-notes; Latin songs play them straight; Nashville melodies span an octave or less; Broadway melodies span an octave and more. Each style, though, is more than its specifics. Song styles spring from rich traditions. Appalachian folk songs come from Scottish and Irish ballads, the blues from slave hollers and work songs, and gospel songs come from hymns and spirituals. Jazz songs have a tradition now a century old, from ragtime to Dixieland to swing to bebop to fusion. Rock 'n' roll's tradition is already fifty years young, from Chuck Berry to Buddy Holly to Phil Spector to The Beatles to The Grateful Dead to Madonna. Tap into these song style traditions, and you'll get the benefit of their unique flavors, the way they color and convey emotion.

Even untutored listeners recognize many song styles and respond to them at different moments and moods in their lives. Rock 'n' roll wakes up Charley on the morning commute, easy listening lulls him at work, and redneck C&W gets him pounding the dashboard on the way home. Kathy likes to spin CDs by Carole King or Joni Mitchell at home, but when she goes out dancing, she wants a dreamy samba band. If you write a song in a definite style, you connect with your listeners on a well-established wavelength. Your song, though new, has outlines already familiar.

How can you learn song styles well enough to catch their essence in your writing? Listen. Now is the time for spinning around the radio dial as I suggested in the first chapter, the time to buy CDs by artists in styles you've never listened to before. Here's a much too short list of songwriters with (I apologize) tags identifying their styles:

Fats Waller	swing jazz
Cole Porter	Broadway
Willie Dixon	blues
Johnny Cash	country
Carl Perkins	rockabilly
Thelonious Monk	bebop
Curtis Mayfield	rhythm & blues
Crosby, Stills, and Nash	folk rock
Phil Spector	rock 'n' roll
Jagger–Richards	rock blues
Antonio Carlos Jobim	bossa nova

Smokey Robinson	Motown
George Clinton	funk
Bob Marley	reggae
Barry White	disco
Beck	90s rock
Tupac Shakur	rap

Study as well as listen. Get songbooks by these and other songwriters across a wide stylistic spectrum. Play their songs, feel their rhythms, analyze their chord structures, and sing their melodies and lyrics. How do they do what they do? How do they use their musical tools to hammer together a song? What identifies their style?

As you start to glimpse the mechanics behind the magic, imitate. I don't mean dead-on copy or plagiarize; that's a no-no and a dead-end. I do mean trying to write songs in these styles, consciously modeling your work on what appeals to you in the original. For example, I've long loved the great Holland–Dozier–Holland song, "Heatwave," and years ago I got a Motown book and learned it, always enjoying this chord sequence that gives the song such lift:

Example 94

A few months later I felt a song coming on about young love; "Boys and Girls," I called it. The new song seemed to need an upbeat Motown style, and I found myself playing "Heatwave." "Yeah," I thought, "I want this song to sound like that." A few hours pounding away on my guitar and I had the structure of "Boys and Girls." Lo and behold, it did sound like a Motown song, and the chorus had those "Heatwave" chords, but in reverse:

Example 95

Try playing a few standards in new styles—"You Are My Sunshine" jazz-style, "Take the A Train" country-style—and see what you learn. Play your own songs in new styles, rewriting as necessary, and feel how they fit their new skins. Remember that finding a song's style is a creative process just like finding its chords, melodies, and forms. If a song begins as a rock song, hard and bouncy, then morphs into something soft and jazzy, follow where the song takes you. Every songwriter's goal is to suit the style to the song so both unite in expressing the song's core emotion. Painting a Brazilian twilight with punk rock or a Michigan trailer park with a bossa nova might not work, unless you're writing a comedy song, and that's a rich and varied style all its own.

Story

The word "story," *historia* in ancient Greek and Latin, is among the oldest and most potent words in our language. We all know what a story is, of course, but let's take a fresh look at the word and what it means.

All about and inside us life seethes with ceaseless change. The tiny corner of life each of us gets to see is immense: our inner selves, our families and friends, our home, neighborhood, town, city, state, country, planet, and starry sky. A moment of reflection reveals that everything in our lives connects with everything else in our lives, that the places, people, and happenings we experience are connected to each other by an infinite number of crisscross links, some visible like roads and electric wires, some invisible like thought, memory, and imagination. These links create the fabric we live in, the network of human and natural activity humming with the vibrations of its zillion billion nodes, each node sending, receiving, and responding to signals, and every signal, though sent in certain directions, radiating through the entire network, influencing nodes thousands of miles and thousands of years away. All this goes on as one day rolls through night to the new day, the surge of life ebbing and flowing but always going on, a great river with no beginning or end, an ocean with no shores.

Life this vast intrigues but overwhelms the human mind. We have always struggled to put boundless life into shapes we can contemplate and use, to make life make sense. In life's endlessness, we've learned to see patterns and rhythms, beginnings and endings, sunrise and sunset, birth and death. We can select single events in the life-flow and see how one event causes the next. We can detach a few events, places, and people from the universal background and bring them up to the foreground, start them at a one point in time, watch (or imagine) what happens to them until another point in time, and then relate to other humans what we observed (or imagined) happening. That "telling of a happening or a connected series of happenings," says the dictionary, is a story.

Stories come in all shapes, sizes, and lengths. The Bible, Shakespeare's plays, and Dickens' novels tell long stories woven from the lives of many characters. O. Henry wrote short stories woven from the lives of two or three characters. The shortest stories I know are these two from a wise Chinese proverb: "Father dies, son dies: happy story. Son dies, father dies: sad story." Poems and plays tell stories. Paintings, sculptures, dance, and mime tell stories without words. Songs tell stories with words and music. Stories take so many forms that it's hard to say what makes a story, but I find three elements are indispensable: a beginning and an ending, specific description, and a revelation about life.

This is not a story:

> A man came running down the street, his clothes disheveled, a terrified look on his face. He burst through the door of his house and shouted to his wife, "Guess what just happened!"

Its unresolved suspense denies us a satisfying ending. Neither is this a story:

> A man, I think his name was Bob, but it might have been Jack because his father was named Jack and I think he was a junior, anyway, Jack's, or Bob's, brother told me that after Stella went to the movies, someone came to their house, and they asked him to dinner. I'm not sure if he stayed or not.

It's too vague. This is a minimal story:

> A woman ate her dinner then read a book.

but what it reveals about life is commonplace.

This is a story:

> Feeling lonely, Joe decided to get a pet. At the store he told the clerk that he wanted an unusual pet. "Centipedes make nice pets," said the clerk, so Joe bought a centipede and took it home in a little house-shaped box.
>
> After putting the box on a sunny shelf, Joe thought he'd start their friendship by taking his new pal out for a drink. So he whispered into the box, "Would you like to go to Frank's with me and have a beer?"
>
> The centipede did not answer.

This bothered Joe, but he waited a few minutes then asked again nicely, "How about going to the bar and having a drink with me?"

Again no answer from the centipede.

Now Joe was annoyed, so he put his face up against a window in the box and shouted, "Hey, you in there! Wanna go to Frank's place for a damn beer?"

This time a little voice came out of the box: "I heard you the first time! I'm putting on my goddamn shoes!"

This story begins and moves to a satisfying ending, describes a definite world (though there's much we don't learn: Joe's last name, where he lives, how old he is, or how much he paid for his pet), and it reveals, amusingly, the idiot impatience of human nature.

Songs and storytelling are inextricably linked. The first storytellers discovered that melody and rhythm added to their tales and helped their listeners remember the stories longer. Look over a thick book of American songs and you'll see a musical quilt of American history—"Yankee Doodle Dandy," "Dixie," "The Erie Canal," "Home on the Range," "Over There," and "Dust Bowl Blues"—dotted with colorful American characters—"John Henry," "Casey Jones," "Frankie and Johnny," and "Stag-o-lee." The tradition continues with "Fixin' to Die Rag" and "The Ballad of the Green Berets," which tell different stories about the war in Vietnam, and with gangsta stories told by the griots, storytellers, of today's city streets.

Beginning songwriters don't always grasp the song–story connection, and I admit it's easy to miss. Storytelling songs—"Alice's Restaurant" tells how Arlo Guthrie and his pals got arrested for littering in Stockbridge, Massachusetts—can seem a style of songs separate from the many songs that effuse emotion with few story-like details. "Love to Love You, Baby" tells us the singer loves to love Baby but not much else, and doing the Hustle is all that happens in "Do the Hustle."

Yet songs and stories are forever bonded, and here I'll lay down the law: *To live, a song must tell a story*. Good songs tell stories that are as clear and easy to get, each in its own way, as the joke about Joe and his centipede. Wait a minute. What's the story of that nutty masterpiece "I Am the Walrus?" Well, every rule has exceptions, but the rule is: Every song must tell a story. Don't drop everything to write old-timey ballads like "The Battle of New Orleans" ("we fired our guns and the British kept a-coming") or modern story songs like "Tie a Yellow Ribbon 'Round the Old Oak Tree," but do find the story in every song you write.

Look at your latest song as a whole. Does it tell the story you want to tell? Does the story have a beginning and ending, define someone or someplace, reveal an interesting aspect of life? Are your characters consistent or is "I" flippant in the first verse, heartbroken in the second? Does the flow of melody and chords follow the song's emotional curves? Do the tempo and rhythm suit its mood? Have you found a narrative through-line, the common sense logic that will carry listeners through the song just as the joke carried us through Joe going to the pet store and back home? If we jumble up the joke's sentences, we lose the through-line and with it the story.:

> Again the centipede did not answer. At the pet store he told the clerk that he wanted an unusual pet. Feeling lonely, Joe decided to get a pet. So he whispered into the box, "Would you like to go to Frank's with me and have a beer?"

Exactly the same thing can happen to a song whose parts are out of order or whose colors clash.

Still I hear you asking, "Where's the story in a typical June–moon pop song?" tunes. It's true that most pop songs tell not outspoken stories but *oblique stories*, in which the song elements work together to suggest the story with hints and looks and smiles instead of declaring it with dates and times and facts.

Writing oblique story songs poses a challenge for any songwriter. Oblique story songs, like art photographs, tell their tales from odd angles. They cast highlights on a few details and leave others half-hidden in shadow. For example, the opening line of "They Can't Take That Away from Me"—"The way you wear your hat!"—is justly famous for its comic clarity, but how clear is it? Is the hat a flat beret or a flowery bonnet? Does the way she wears it mean at a rakish angle or down low over her eyes? The song doesn't say. "Stormy Weather" tells us a moody story of a lover crying the blues over a long-gone lover, but, despite the sharp rainy day images, much remains vague. Either lover could be of either sex. We never learn how or why the romance ended, nor do we know at the end whether the lovers will ever get back together. "Sophisticated Lady" paints the portrait of a rich, unhappy, but nameless beauty in images both precise—"dancing, dining, diamonds shining"—and blurred—"Out with some man in a restaurant." "Eleanor Rigby's" spare story gives us names and realistic images—Father MacKenzie "wiping his hands as he walked from the grave"—but also surreal images—"the face she keeps in a jar by the door"—and a question mark for an ending—"All the lonely people, where do they all come from?"

The key to writing oblique story songs is to tell as much story as possible with as few specifics as possible. Too many specifics and your story may become too obvious. Too few specifics and your story may fall apart. How many specifics are too many or too few is a matter of taste and the particular song, but try to write so that listeners will feel, not that you are a teacher lecturing them, but a friend sketching an intimate story. Trust that they'll be able to fill in the specifics from their own imaginations. Look for a moment at my "Let's Live Our Love Again":

> A few years,
> A few tears,
> A few gray hairs,
> Look what's become of us!
> Darling, let's live our love again.

> Our first night,
> Candlelight,
> Even our first fight,
> All that's come to us,
> Darling, let's live our love again.

>> Every day with you is so precious,
>> In my heart I store up each and every one,
>> I could love you for a billion years,
>> And at their end be barely begun.

> So who cares,
> 'Bout gray hairs,
> We're still here,
> Whatever comes to us,
> Darling, let's live our love again.

The story is plain enough: a couple looking back over a long, happy marriage, wishing they could live over their years together. The song's easy-going swing beat and "standard" form heighten its nostalgic feeling. I want listeners to see the couple clearly, yet I took pains to keep my images as open-ended as possible: "All that comes to us ... whatever comes to us." In place of "Our first night, candlelight," I first tried "That night in New York" and "Paris in June," then I soon realized that the images would pin down my characters too much and leave out listeners who don't know New York and Paris. But every couple has had a first night, and when I sing "Our first night, candlelight," I'm hoping to evoke in every listening couple fond memories of their own first night together, wherever they were. The lyric works, I think, because when I get to the next line, "Even our first fight," I always get a chuckle of recognition from the crowd. As sweet as that first night was, they know romance is not all champagne and roses.

So before you put down your pencil for good on the new masterpiece, remember: Outspoken or oblique, all good songs tell stories. Everything that helps tell the story, keep. Anything that does not help tell the story, cut. Be ruthless. It may be a fancy flourish that took you weeks to work out, a lyric that gives you goosebumps, or a cool hook you stole from a big hit, but if it gets in the way of the story . . . see you later, alligator.

chapter 10

Chord Structures—Part II

In *Chord Structures—Part I*, I asked you to remember *scale tone triads*. Let's come back to these triads as a starting point to develop our chord structures and their endless expressive possibilities.

Here again are the scale tone triads in the key of C major:

Example 96 Track Six

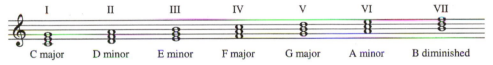

These triads are the building blocks of chord structure; they carry our melodies and make our song forms go round and round. By now we're old hands with I, IV, and V, the C major, F major, and G major triads, but before going on to the chords we're less familiar with, let's take another look at V. In numerous examples, I've already shown V as G7, which means the triad adds a fourth note, F, on top:

Example 97 Track Six

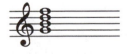

Why G7? Why in any key is V usually written as V7?

The biggest tonal movement in music, remember, is from I to V and back to I. When V goes to the I, the dominant resolves into the tonic (the third of the string falls back into the whole string). If I'm playing a song in C and come to a G chord before a final C, I can feel that V headed to its I so strongly that it seems to tilt toward its goal. If, while playing the G chord, I lower my top G to an F, and then go on to E when the C chord arrives, I feel that I'm increasing G's tilt into C:

Example 98 Track Six

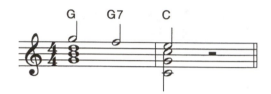

That is why songbooks nearly always show the V chord written as V7. The seventh helps push the V chord toward I. The seventh, as I tell my students, is an *added color.* It is not absolutely necessary. Start using the seventh, though, and you'll soon find the unadorned V triad bland.

Now we move on to the II, III, VI and VII chords. We'll begin with VII, both the trickiest and the least important, which we can get out of the way with a brief word. Neither major nor minor, VII is *a diminished chord*, which means that both its mediant and its dominant have been pulled down a half-step from their positions in B major:

Example 99 Track Six

Diminished chords are wonderful, useful chords with a spooky, melodramatic sound, but, to skip their intricacies, let's look again at that B diminished chord. What does its B, D, F remind you of? Yes, a G7 chord without the G. Diminished chords are most often used as V7 chords without the root, so here we'll call VII a variant of V. You may discover more about diminished chords on your own.

II, III, and VI are all minor chords, their mediants a half-step lower than a major chord's mediant. That small change gives minor chords more pastel colors than a major chord's bold red-white-and-blue. II, III, and VI do not have I, IV, and V's structural importance. These chords live in the open space between the posts and beams of tonic, subdominant, and dominant:

Example 100

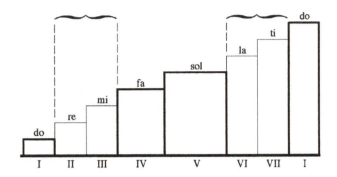

Start mixing II, III, and VI chords among your I, IV, and V in a few eight-bar songs. Play these three and others you invent, and hear how these new chords affect the music:

Example 101 Track Six

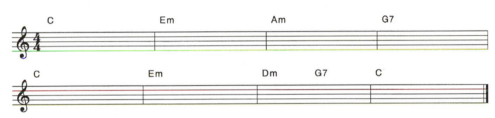

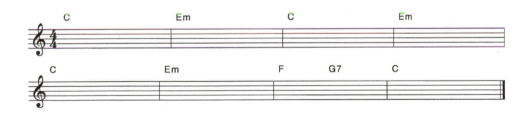

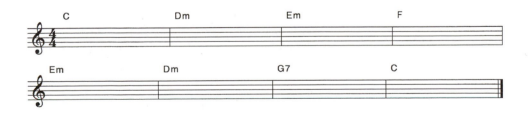

Overall, II, III, and VI soften the sharp edges of I, IV, and V. They bridge gaps between the structural chords, and they smooth the flow of a sequence that otherwise might sound stop-and-go.

II and VI have featured roles in one of music's most common chord sequences, I–VI–II–V:

Example 102 Track Six

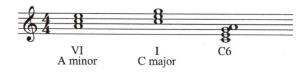

Play and sing I–VI–II–V over and over again in all keys and at all tempos, in three-four and four-four time. Do everything you can to get the sequence into your ears, voice, hands, and bones. I–VI–II–V is the heart of many pieces by Haydn and Mozart and many pop standards like "I Got Rhythm," "Heart and Soul," "Blue Moon," and "Stormy Weather." It is also the heart of the "doo-wop" songs of early rock 'n' roll like "Earth Angel," "The Duke of Earl," "Silhouettes," and "Dream." Songwriters love I–VI–II–V songs for their melodic, conversational curves. Singers and jazz players love them because they are easy to harmonize and improvise on. Listeners love them for their relaxed, familiar swing. May you write a dozen great I–VI–II–V songs.

Why is I–VI–II–V such a beloved chord structure? We could fill a book with reasons, but here are two. First, I–VI–II–V is really a disguised form of I–V. We can consider A minor a variant of C major (the top two tones are C–E), and if we moved the A from the bottom of A minor to the top of C major, then we've got C sixth:

Example 103

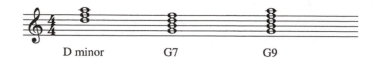

Likewise, we can consider II a variant of V (D minor and G7 have D–F in common, and D minor's A can be added on top of G7 to make G9):

Example 104

If we don't use the variants and play I–VI–II–V as I–I–V–V, we go back to the boxy sound of a plain tonic-dominant progression. By using II and VI, we get both the strength of I–V and the grace of chords gliding easily into each other:

Example 105 Track Six

The second reason for I–VI–II–V's popularity is that the structure gives us a powerful sequence of chord roots (C to A to D to G and back to C):

Example 106 Track Six

The roots start on C at the bottom of the C major triad, which then moves to its sixth, A, to make the closely related chord, A minor. Now notice that, from A onward, the roots keep going V to I: A is the V of D, D is the V of G, and G is the V of C (one dominant-to-tonic resolution after another). I–VI–II–V, in a word, keeps going home, and each home turns into a way station for the next home. We make the small change from C major to A minor to get a bass note that will get the V–I daisy chain started, and, once started, around and around we go.

To sense I–VI–II–V's dog-chasing-its-tail effect, try playing and singing the sequence starting on II:

Example 107 Track Six

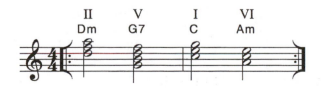

This way the sequence develops so much momentum that you'll never want to put on the brakes with a final I. Here's a melody over II–V–I–VI—a bit like Cole Porter's "I Get a Kick Out of You"—that shows how the off-center structure can give a song an irresistible drive:

Example 108 Track Six

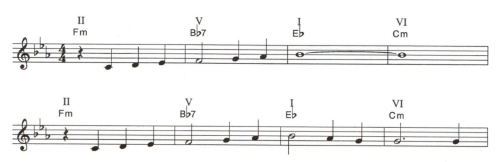

The next step in developing our chord structures is to continue the process we started with C6 and G7, adding tones to the scale tone triads. We can add any tone we like, and every tone brings new colors to the triads. Try out combinations as nutty as your hands and imaginations allow.

Example 109

Adding tones to song chords, however, is not a random process of creating knucklebusters, but a systematic way to give songs new melodies, colors and emotions. Tone adding's basic principle is: go up the scale from the 1–3–5 triad, skipping steps as the triad does. This process is called "moving in thirds" because we are always going to the third step from the one we are on:

Example 110

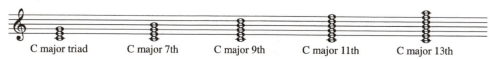

We won't discuss exotics like thirteenth chords, but we will take the small but important step of adding a seventh to all our scale tone triads:

Example 111 Track Six

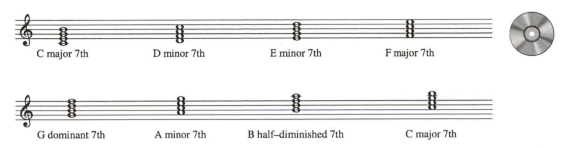

Play these chords and listen to them. Play a simple I–IV–V song using major sevenths for I and IV and a dominant seventh for the V chord. Listen to how it sounds. Sing a la-la melody that brings out the new chord tones. Here's one suggestion:

Example 112 Track Six

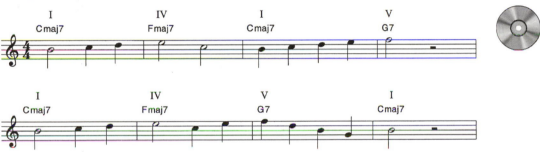

Try the new chords on I–VI–II–V, and sense the new glide they give the sequence:

Example 113 Track Six

Look at the row of seventh chords again, and see how the added seventh multiplies the chord-linking tones we noted in *Chord Structures—Part One*. A few examples: the top of VI, A minor 7, is the C major triad; the top of II, D minor 7, is the IV triad; the bottom three tones of III, E minor 7, are the top three notes of C major 7; and the top three notes of III are the V triad:

Example 114

The more you look, the more linking tones you'll see. As you play the new chords, you'll hear how the added seventh seems to make the chords melt into each other.

If you fall in love with the sound of seventh chords and start using them in your songs, you and your audience will notice the difference. With few exceptions, folk, bluegrass, country and western, and rock songwriters stick to triads, adding a seventh only to the V chord. Major and minor seventh chords will make your songs sound more like "As Time Goes By" than "Tutti Frutti," more Manhattan than Nashville, more George Gershwin than Hank Williams, more Miles Davis than Bob Dylan. For myself, I fell in love years ago with seventh chords and the emotional and musical palette they open up, the subtleties of their links and contrasts, their swirling, glistening swing.

The best way I've found to get the seventh chord sound into my hands and ears is to play the scale tone seventh chords in this sequence, which makes a lovely eight-bar song:

Example 115 Track Six

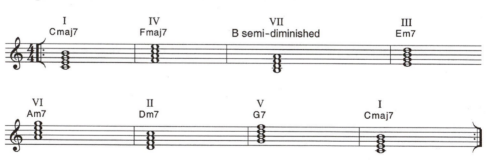

Play this sequence around and around in all keys, singing any melody that springs naturally to mind, and you'll give yourself excellent preparation for playing and writing songs with a jazzy nightclub feeling. Be sure to note that this sequence creates an endless (and almost flawless) daisy chain of V–I root resolutions. C goes to F; then comes the flaw—F goes to B when F is the perfect fifth of B flat. Our ears easily accept the flaw, however, because B is only a half-step off, and because B is in the C major scale that we are sticking to for all our tones. Once we're on that B, then B to E, E to A, A to D, D to

G, and G back to C, it's V–I, V–I, V–I all the way. Moving so steadily around the Circle of Fifths generates a musical momentum both powerful and gentle. As you become familiar with the sequence, you'll recognize this as the force that gives fine standards like "All the Things You Are," "Autumn Leaves," and "Fly Me to the Moon" their insinuating, danceable drive.

There is no end to the subtle alterations we can make to song chord structures, each one adding its unique color and emotion. My problem is to figure out which few to mention here.

We can continue the process we started by adding sevenths, ninths, and elevenths to our triads and using those notes in our melodies:

Example 116

We can add tones to our triads that are not scale tones of the key we're playing in. Jazz songwriters love the V7 chord with the fifth step flatted:

Example 117

An *augmented seventh chord* raises the fifth step of an V7 chord a half-step, further increasing its tilt toward I:

Example 118

A *diminished seventh chord* (see our brief discussion of diminished chords earlier in this chapter) lowers the third, fifth, and seventh steps of a V7 chord:

Example 119

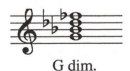

G dim.

Such exotics, however, are not encountered in every song. Far more common is the emphasizing of our old friend, V–I movement, by making a chord a V7 even when its root is not the V of our scale. These chords, called *secondary dominants*, take some explaining, so please focus. We've seen that playing V as V7 adds to V's tilt toward I, and we just looked at a few sequences in which the roots of the chords move V–I, V–I, even though the roots are not the V of the key we're playing in. A minor going to D minor, for example, in I–VI–II–V in C, is VI moving to II at the same time the roots A and D are moving V–I:

Example 120 Track Six

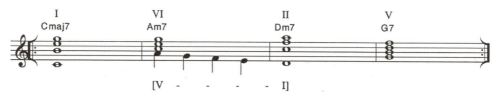

To emphasize this V–I movement at the root of VI–II, we can alter our VI, A minor, into an A dominant seventh, the chord that would occur if we were in the key of D and A was the V in the scale.

Example 121 Track Six

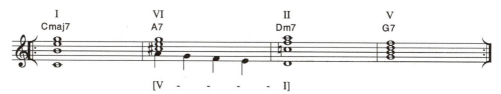

Play I–VI–II–V with this alteration, and see how it sounds. G7 is the primary dominant because G is the V of the whole song's scale, but A7 is a secondary dominant, acting for its measure like a true V chord. In effect, we have modulated briefly into the key of D minor. Back in *Chord Structures—Part I*, we saw that we could turn a I at the end of an A section into a temporary V7 to modulate into the key of the IV for the bridge:

Example 122 Track Six

The modulation can also happen within an A section. The chord structures for the A sections of "Ain't Misbehavin'," "Smoke Gets in Your Eyes," and many other songs are identical: I–VI–II–V for two measures, then a brief modulation into the key of the IV using I7 as a secondary dominant, then going back to more I–VI–II–V:

Example 123 Track Six

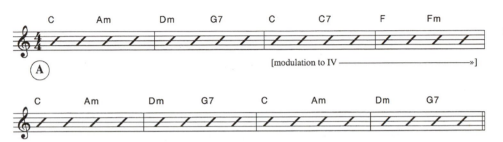

In "Your Cheating Heart," Hank Williams gets to his bridge in F by using the old C–C7 ploy, then he uses a D7 chord as a secondary dominant to modulate briefly into the key of G. G7, the primary dominant, takes us back into C for another A section:

Example 124 Track Six

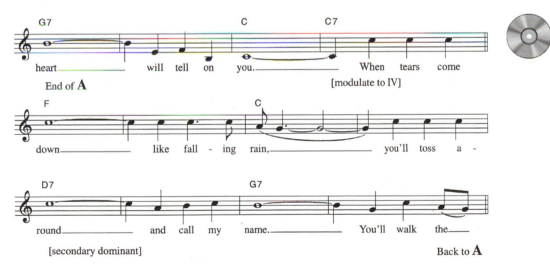

Why do we bother with the long names of these chord alterations and their brain-twisting rationales? We bother because altered chords give us sound colors and shapes we can get no other way. Altered chords can smooth out *voice leading*, the progression of a melody note to note. A diminished seventh, for example, can connect I and II seamlessly:

Example 125

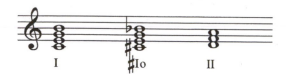

The C–C7–F–F minor–C sequence above from "Ain't Misbehavin'" and other songs allows a long chromatic (in half-steps) run from C down to G:

Example 126

The blues alters chords in so many unique and slippery ways that the subject could fill a whole book. In essence, the blues shapes its I–IV–V basics to bring out the "blue notes" of the *pentatonic blues scale*:

Example 127 Track Six

That five-tone scale encourages us to play I, IV, and V as dominant seventh chords and gives us many ways to create the major–minor ambiguity that gives the blues its distinctive color:

Example 128 Track Six

Technical analysis of chord alterations becomes brain-numbing past a certain point. New chords are more fun to play than to study! So I'll conclude with two reminders to bring us back to basics:

- Alter chords only if the new chords help you say what you want to say. Each new chord has new colors, and we songwriters are lucky to have this multi-hued musical paintbox to paint our multi-hued inner lives. Yet play in the paintbox with a purpose. Using exotic chords to show off how cool you are is a dead-end street. Sometimes, I know, a regular old V7 won't do, you must have an augmented seventh's sweet poignancy, but when in doubt, keep it simple.

- As you paint with chord colors, remember construction. Beneath the skin of complex songs stand tonic, subdominant, and dominant skeletons much like in "Oh, Susanna." Never forget that skeleton. The I–IV–V folk song is like an old-fashioned chair, sturdy and plain, and a jazz tune with far-out chords is like modern easy chair, curvy and fancy:

We may admire the modern chair's ingenuity, but if we plan to sit on it, those curves had better be hiding a structure as sturdy as the chair's, or we'll fall flat on our butts.

chapter 11

Lyrics—Part II

In our first chapter on the subject, we found only one rule for writing lyrics: lyrics must say something. Let's start to build on that rock-bottom to look further into the art. What your lyrics say is up to you. Here are a few ideas on how to get it said.

First of all, be concise. People don't mind oratorical flourishes from podium or pulpit, but in art and daily life, listeners apply a steady pressure on speakers to get to the point. Good lyrics are concise. Most speak their piece in fifty to one hundred words, and few need more than two hundred. As important as overall length is interior concision. Even an epic saga like "The Ballad of Davy Crockett" can't afford to waste a syllable. Nearly every lyric boils down its hundred-plus words into a one-, two-, three-, four-, or five-word phrase, often repeated, that contains the concentrated essence of what the lyric has to say.

Finding these few words is of utmost importance when mulling over a new song. Like actors who can't get into a character until they find the right hat or the right tie, many lyricists get into a song only when some happy inspiration delivers the memorable phrase that says it all. A few years ago I was fumbling for a song to suit the '30s jazz sound of a new band I had joined. Joking with Ellen one day, I said, "Tell me lies." "Hey," I thought a second later, "that's usable." In a week I had a new Billie Holiday-style ballad called "Tell Me Lies":

> I know you're leaving, comes as no surprise,
> I've seen that long gone look deep in your eyes
> But darling tonight, shut out the light,
> Tell me lies....

Here, as often happens, my few words became the song's title. That's why many old pros advise beginners, "Find your title first." Yet "title" sounds like a label stuck on the outside of a lyric. These few words are the core of a lyric, the seed from which the lyric grows. Let's call our crucial few words the lyric's *heart-phrase*, a name that better suggests its value.

Think of the heart-phrase of a half-dozen songs you love. In my random half-dozen—"Yesterday," "Georgia on My Mind," "Ain't Misbehavin'," "Hey Good Looking," "Blowing in the Wind," "I Could Have Danced All Night"—the barebones titles often need a few words to make the full phrase—"Hey good-looking, whatcha got cooking?" "The answer is blowing in the wind." Notice that all the heart-phrases encompass the entire image the lyric conveys. Every word of "Yesterday" is about near-and-yet-so-far yesterday, every word of "Georgia on my Mind" about near-and-yet-so-far Georgia. Bob Dylan's wind whispers answers to all his questions. "I could have danced all night," sings a girl reeling with the joys of music and champagne and whirling in her lover's arms.

Once you find your heart-phrase, where do you set it? A heart-phrase can be the first words of a lyric, as in *"Somewhere over the rainbow*, way up high...". It can be the last words of the A section:

> I tell my friends that I don't care,
> I shrug my shoulders at the whole affair,
> But they all know, it isn't so,
> I'm foolin' myself.

or it can be the repeated refrain of the chorus: "I remember mama said—*You can't hurry love*."

Wherever it falls, everything else in the lyric must flow from the heart-phrase and lead to the heart-phrase. All must support and amplify the heart-phrase. Let's look at the complete lyric of "Foolin' Myself." In the first A section "I" describes trying to fool him or herself.

> I tell myself I'm through with love,
> I'll have nothing more to do with love,
> I stay away, but every day,
> I'm foolin' myself.

In the second A section "I" is trying to fool other people:

> I tell my friends that I don't care,
> I shrug my shoulders at the whole affair,

But they all know, it isn't so,
I'm foolin' myself.

In the bridge he or she takes a look in the mirror and sees a fool:

Every time I pass
And see myself in the looking glass,
I tip my hat and say,
"How do you do, you fool,
You're throwing your life away."

In the last A "I" is still acting up a storm to no avail:

I act gay, I act proud,
And every time I see you in a crowd,
I pretend, but in the end,
I'm just foolin' myself.

"I" has fooling on the brain. Not for a second does the lyric swerve from the heart-phrase's stated purpose to show someone trying and failing to fool themselves. If "I" had digressed to talk about cheering, comforting, or lecturing, then the lyric would have been greatly weakened. The strength of this lyric springs from "I"'s total focus on "fooling myself." Keep your lyrics this close to their heart-phrase.

Who is this "I?" "I" is whoever sings the lyric. We songwriters are our own first "I," and we hope that listeners and other singers will recognize our "I" as a human being who has emotions and ideas that they can understand and with whom they can sympathize. We hope "I" is a person they could be themselves, in their own way.

Being true to yourself is the first step in creating a believable "I," but not the only step. Creating the "I" of a lyric is a subtle matter, much like creating the performing persona we discussed above. A lyricist may write two songs back-to-back, one creating a brokenhearted boyfriend doomed to despair, the next a Mr. Happy-Go-Lucky, head over heels in love. Which is he? Both. When writing or singing a lyric, we play a role, take on a character. As I learn a new song, either an original or a standard, I feel that I'm wrapping the cloak of another personality over my shoulders, taking on a voice, posture, and point of view that are new to me. The song is a one-act play. I'm the actor, and the lyrics are my lines. "I" is me, but a special me crafted to suit the song, that brings out aspects of me that otherwise might lie dormant, unexplored, or unexpressed.

Let this acting magic steal over you as you write lyrics. With the heart-phrase that got you started may have come images of the person who's singing the song and where that "I" is singing it. Let such images blossom in your mind. See your "I." How old and how well-dressed is "I?" See the "you" "I" is singing to. Are these people outdoors, indoors, or in bed? Is it morning, noon, or night? What has just happened between them that makes "I" sing this song to "you?" Soon, instead of stringing words together to fill out lines and rhymes, you'll be talking in a character's voice, choosing words and expressions they would choose, sketching the world they're living in.

Making such an organic connection to a lyric's *subtext*, the complex drama that underlies its few words, can enrich your work beyond measure. Jimmy Webb's "By The Time I Get to Phoenix" leaps to mind as a song that vividly creates character and setting: a guy rolling on a bus east across Arizona, farther and farther from his girl. In his masterpiece, "One for My Baby (And One More for the Road)," Johnny Mercer needs only a few sure strokes to place his "I," another lonely guy, in an empty bar deep in the wee hours: "It's quarter to three, there's no one in the place except you and me . . .".

As you explore your lyric's subtext, remember that you don't need to word-paint every image you think of. The "I" of most pop lyrics is an everyman or woman who is feeling a particular emotion but is not a particular person in a particular setting. Why? Because pop lyricists try not hem in their "I" with biographical details. They want millions of people to identify with "I" soul-to-soul instead of thinking, "She's not me; she's a Las Vegas showgirl."

Only in opera or Broadway-style musicals must every line of a lyric convey a specific character's response to plot twists and turns. For a musical of *Death of a Salesman*, you'll have to write lyrics to suit an over-the-hill shoe salesman in New York with a loyal wife and two no-good sons. Writing lyrics for show songs is a fine goal, but one beyond the scope of this book. We singer–song-writers can take a more freeform approach to character and setting. It's worth noting, however, that the best show lyricists, by conscious design, fit their lyrics to the show *and* give them everyman appeal. Often show song lyrics open with a *verse*, a brief semi-sung recitative, that smoothes the transition from the show's story line to a song anyone could sing. In "I Could Have Danced All Night," for example, "I" is Eliza Doolittle, the cockney heroine of *My Fair Lady*, just home from her first fancy-dress ball. Henry Higgins tells her it's time for bed, and she replies, speak-singing:

Bed! Bed! I couldn't go to bed!
My head's too light to try to set it down!

Sleep! Sleep! I couldn't sleep tonight!
Not for all the jewels in the crown!

Then she launches into song, "I could have danced all night."

To create a believable "I" in a believable setting, all the experts advise using vivid images, words that paint precise pictures of the people and places you want the listener to see. I agree. That's what I'm trying for in my lyrics, and that's what I love about songs like "These Foolish Things," which give us snap-shot glances into the world of the singer and the song: "A cigarette that bears a lipstick's traces, An airline ticket to romantic places ..."

Yet remember too the value of mystery to lyrics. Hints, metaphors, and even downright vagueness can say as much in a lyric as precision. Examples from nearly every good lyric will prove the point—just above, for instance, the sharp pictures of "These Foolish Things" flow into a magic image: "My heart has wings." The A sections of "Georgia on My Mind," show us the "moonlight through pines" clearly, but the bridge—"Other arms reach out to me / Other eyes smile tenderly"—moves us into a dreamy world where bodiless but sexy sirens swirl around "I," tempting "I" to stray from the straight-and-narrow. One of my songs, "Love at First Sight," paints a couple remembering the night they met dancing to the music of a swing band at a lakeside casino adorned with Chinese lanterns. In the bridge, "I" comments:

By now we've had a while to look each other,
We've seen what time can bring to lovers ...

"Well, that's pretty vague," complained one singer when I played her the song. "What *does* time bring to lovers? Give me an image." Her critique made me think, but I didn't change a word. Having sung the lyric countless times, I'm convinced that the vagueness of "what time can bring" gives me the room to pour the joys and sorrows my wife and I have known into how I sing the line. Audience response likewise tells me that listening couples fill the vague-ness with whatever time has brought them.

Recommending both precision and mystery leads to a rich but seldom mentioned resource for lyric writing: *opposites.*

Combining opposite words—called *oxymoron* when the opposites are beside each other like, "cold fire, sick health" (Shakespeare), and *antithesis* when close in balanced phrases like, "I hate and I love" (Ovid)—is one of writing's most ancient devices. Combined opposites create checkerboard contrasts that readers instantly sense and long remember. Dickens' "It was the best of times, it was the worst of times. . . ," may be the most famous opening lines in literature. Opposites organize what we say and sort out a mixed bag of events, for example, "I've got good news and bad news." They also expand what we say. "I searched high and low" means we also searched everywhere in-between. Combining opposites goes deeper than word play. Life pulls together opposite words—hot and cold, happy and sad, young and old, alive and dead—to describe the opposite experiences we know, for good or ill, from living in our world. War and peace, winter and summer, man and woman—how curiously are these linked, each one, for all its stubborn independence, complementing the other, melting into each other, needing the other to exist.

It's no accident, therefore, that opposites find their way into daily speech—"open and shut case," "sweet and sour sauce"—and into lyrics like "First you say you will, and then you won't," "Sometimes I'm happy, sometimes I'm blue," "If, baby, I'm the bottom, you're the top." I've long loved the old blues lyric:

> You may be high, you may be low,
> You may be rich, you may be poor,
> But when the Lord gets ready,
> You got to move.

Note how in "Tears of a Clown" Smokey Robinson crisscrosses happy and sad opposites with alone and with-others opposites:

> *Smiling* in the *public* eye,
> But in my *lonely* room I *cry*
> The tears of a clown.

Frank Loesser sets "She" and "He" opposite each other in "Baby, It's Cold Outside" and supports their battle of the sexes with the parallel opposition of winter without and warmth within.

> She: The answer is no!
> He: But baby it's cold outside
> She: The welcome has been...
> He: How lucky that you dropped in!
> She: So nice and warm.
> He: Look out the window at that storm.

Look over your lyrics for opposites. You'll find many that you've used just because they worked, and you'll find murky passages that a good opposite will clear up. Opposites can be bigger than paired images. For example, contrasting the mood of the bridge lyric with the mood of the A section lyrics builds opposition into your song structure. In my "Made It to Another Spring," the A's beam with birds and bees and budding flowers, while the bridge looks somberly back to a tough winter:

> There were times in the winter
> When I didn't think we'd make it through
> Hell of a storm at New Year's,
> Little Billy got a hell of a flu ...

Opposites show us life "from both sides now," as one good lyric put it, and help us write lyrics true to life's contradictions. A lyric's big statement may be "Love makes me happy," but unless we can also suggest that love sometimes make us sad, we'll sound like idiots out of touch with reality. Let your ups and your downs into your lyrics, and you'll do much to convince listeners that you are a human as silly and serious as they, living in the same topsy-turvy world.

Though lyrics can say anything we lyricists dream up to say, I've found over a lifetime of listening that nearly all lyrics, in varying proportions and combinations, touch on three major themes: *music, humor,* and *love.*

Many good lyrics—more than you might think—refer to music one way or another. Start with the countless songs that have the sound of music in their titles—"Seventy-Six Trombones," "I Hear a Symphony"—add to them the countless dance songs—"Begin the Beguine," "The Tennessee Waltz,"—then pile on top the countless songs in which "I" is a singer—"I Let a Song Go Out of My Heart," "I Gotta Right to Sing the Blues,"—and you'll get a goodly percentage of the pop tunes from the last one hundred years.

All kinds of music get into lyrics. "The Trolley Song" makes music from city sounds in the good old days before automobiles: "Clang, clang, clang, went the trolley / Ding, ding, ding, went the bell ..." "Maybellene" captures "the highway sound" of a roaring V-8 Ford. Paeans to birdsong are perennial items in lyrics: "A Nightingale Sang in Berkeley Square," "Skylark," "Rockin' Robin." Many lyrics that we don't think of as being about music slip musical images in among their visual images. Looking at the snapshots in "These Foolish Things," we hear "a tinkling piano in the next apartment."

Like a play within a play or a movie about making a movie, lyrics about music create a curious but powerful doubling effect. The lyric is talking about itself, seeing itself in the mirror. Singers love lyrics about music and singing because the doubling effect adds a challenging new level of meaning and emotion to work with. Try singing, "I'm eating in the rain," then sing, "I'm singing in the rain," and you'll feel the extra gusto of the second.

Welcome music into your lyrics. Write a song about the music you love ("And That's Jazz!" or "It's Only Rock 'n' Roll But I Like It"), your instrument ("My Guitar Gently Weeps" or "Baby Grand"), or about a musician ("Boogie-Woogie Bugle Boy" or "Johnny B. Goode"). As you create the setting and mood of a love song, be on the lookout for musical images like a cafe jukebox playing a country tune or an accordion on a street corner in Paris. No need to bend a lyric out of shape, but if a sound image of any kind pops up—a train whistle at night, a slammed door, your lover's footsteps echoing down the stairs and out of your life—try to work it in.

The lyric you're writing now may be a masterpiece as bleak as "Strawberry Fields Forever" or "I Wish It Would Rain," but once you're done, remember that most pop songs are humorous and say what they say with a smile.

Why do pop song comedies outnumber tragedies? First of all, songwriters tend to be devil-may-care troubadours, guys and gals who cheerfully go where music takes them, who accept the bad with the good and do their best to keep a twinkle in their eyes, a song on their lips. Glance over any list of song titles—"Life is Just a Bowl of Cherries," "Put on a Happy Face," "Blue Skies," "Everything's Coming Up Roses"—and you'll soon sense the cockeyed optimism that pervades the songwriter state of mind. We singer–songwriters can count ourselves lucky. We've learned that we can sing our blues away, that the pleasures of music make stout weapons against fear and despair. We enjoy raising our voices to spread the gospel of taking a positive attitude toward life, of directing our feet "to the sunny side of the street."

Second, even if you're an unrelenting sourpuss, you'll need to write humorous songs because humans like humorous songs. Frazzled by the daily grind, worried about paying the rent and bringing the kids up right, people look to pop music for entertainment and encouragement. They turn on the radio or put on a disc to brighten up a boring workday. They go out to clubs and concerts at night to let the good times roll. Yes, they enjoy a sad song now and then, "Going Down Slow" or "Yesterday," but just as movie-goers prefer happy endings, pop music fans prefer lyrics that make them laugh, that renew their hopes. As part of the great social contract that holds our world together, the public strikes a rough-and-ready bargain with songwriters and other entertainers: "Our jobs are being schoolteachers, farmers, and accountants, and it ain't easy. Your job is helping us forget our troubles, not adding to them."

How can you get humor into your lyrics? As always, observe life. Keep your eyes open and ears cocked, and you'll soon collect dozens of absurd incidents or quirky insights itching for lyrics that'll make listeners giggle or guffaw as you did at the original.

Trust your sense of humor, a precious inborn quality at the core of your personality, as unique as your fingerprints. You may love slapstick, custard pies and fart balloons, your best friend may love stiff-upper-lip comedy, veddy-veddy British, and neither of you could say why exactly. They just make you laugh.

Build on your sense of humor. Quite likely you'll write best in the comic style that most tickles your fancy. That may be storytelling humor like the embarrassing adventures of "A Boy Named Sue." Or it may be satire like the boring letters kids write home from camp in "Hello Mudder, Hello Fadder." Or it could be urbane irony like the murderous socialite of "Miss Otis Regrets," or sketch comedy like the two old tomcats of "We Didn't See a Thing" who meet on the prowl late one night, winking and grinning as they get their stories straight: "I didn't see you / You didn't see me / We didn't see a thing!"

Play with your words, let them loose to play with each other. "Shuffle off to Buffalo," "It's been a hard day's night," "See you later, alligator, in a while, crocodile"—there's something funny about word sounds and word meanings colliding and careening off each other at crazy angles. Come up with wordplay as undeniably cute as Irving Caesar's "Tea for two, and two for tea / Me for you and you for me," and people will be singing your lyric in a hundred years as they still are singing his.

Like jokes, funny lyrics aim to make us lose control in laughter but are themselves set in time-honored structures that lead us step-by-step from the setup through suspense to the punchline's surprise. Like countless classic "priest, minister, and rabbi" jokes, Leonard Feather's "How Blue Can You Get" lyric opens with a three-line setup that B.B. King has been singing for forty years:

> I gave you a brand new Ford, you said "I want a Cadillac,"
> I let you live in my penthouse, you said it was just a shack,
> I bought you a four-course dinner, you said thanks for the
>   snack . . .

Every time the audience's chuckle swells louder with each line, but when B.B. gets to the killer last line, that's when the crowd explodes into laughter:

> I gave you seven children, and now you want to give 'em back,

A few out-and-out comedy songs—"The Chipmunk Song," "The Purple People-Eater," "Transfusion"—become long-remembered *novelty song* hits. More common are lyrics laced with humor though their overall mood may be serious and sincere. Ira Gershwin brilliantly interwove witty words and romantic rhapsodies. The soft smile of "s'wonderful, s'marvelous, that you should care for me" adds sweetness to the sentiment. "Embraceable You," a passionate, tear-in-the eye ballad, has this nutty rhyme that always gets a laugh:

> Just one look at you, and my heart grew *tipsy in me*,
> You and you alone bring out the *gypsy in me*.

Listen twice to many sad songs, and you'll hear a comic spirit opposing, even defying the gloom. In "Good Morning Heartache" a woman wakes at dawn weighed down with troubles. The blues she thought she'd beaten the night before are still staring her in the face, but she stares back and by the end she's making cautious friends with her old enemy: "I guess I better get used to you hanging around / Good morning, heartache, sit down."

The "I" of my "Tell Me Lies" feels deeply wounded that his girl is leaving, but he fights back with cynical humor:

> Put your arms around me, whisper in my ear,
> Maybe you could work up one phony tear,
> Make 'em outrageous, make 'em contagious,
> Tell me lies.

Need I mention that such light moments in heavy songs make welcome opposites? Make one goal of your lyrics blending the comic and the tragic so poignantly that listeners do not know, when tears start in their eyes, whether they're crying from sadness or from joy.

"What is this thing called love?" Cole Porter asked seventy years ago. Don't look at me. I don't have the answer. For the good of lyric writing, however, I'll dare a few remarks.

Love is an emotion, a feeling that stirs the heart and soul of nearly every human being. We may well pity any among us untouched by love. We can love any person we know, father and mother, wife and husband, brother and sister, son and daughter. The circles of love expand through every degree of family and friendly relation to millions of people we don't know who live at far ends of the earth. We can love our home, our hometown, our home country, and our home planet with its beauties of the passing seasons, the animals two-by-two, the mountains and oceans, the stars and silver moon. We can love our work and our play, our cat and the neighbor's dog, a good book, a glass of wine with bread and cheese, and we can love a good night's sleep so much that we can sing with Irving Berlin, "I hate to get up, I hate to get up, I hate to get up in the morning."

If love pervades our lives, our music-making cannot escape its influence. Music and love have been married too long ever to be put asunder. No one could spend the days, weeks, months, and years needed to learn singing, playing, and writing songs without loving music itself, its sounds and colors and sensual pleasures, nor without loving music's ability to embody the love we feel inside and communicate it to others, to create soul-stirring experiences that bring people together to share openhearted love with each other.

Love lives in the piping melodies of a piccolo and the boom-boom rhythms of a big bass drum, and love certainly lives in lyrics. Most lyrics describe how, and how much, somebody loves somebody else. Lyrics proclaim love of music, as we've seen, love of God ("He's Got the Whole World in His Hands"), love of country ("God Bless America"), love of food ("Peanut Butter"), love of seasons ("Summertime"), love of places ("New York, New York"), and love of sports ("Take Me Out to the Ballgame"), yet loved somebodies are the subject of the vast majority of songs. Lyrics have painted every shade of love between humans, from friendship ("such a perfect blendship," wrote Irving Berlin), to passion ("You give me fever," wrote Willie John), to undying devotion ("I'm gonna love you, like nobody loved you, come rain or come shine" wrote Johnny Mercer).

A few pop lyrics, like "M-O-T-H-E-R Spells Mother to Me" or "He Ain't Heavy, He's My Brother," describe parent-child or sibling love, but most describe man–woman love, and not cool platonic love, but hot erotic love, love fueled by physical desire, love raw and romantic, tremulous and tender, nervous and needy. Lovers feel the subtlest shifts in passion's tone and color with overwhelming intensity. They seek fulfillment in sexual pleasure but do not always find their bed of roses. Love frustrated can turn ugly and wears jealousy, rage, shame, and hate among its many masks.

To capture romance's ruby-red shades, as precisely as agonized lovers feel them, is any lyricist's greatest challenge. We've discussed getting emotions into our lyrics. Here's the true test of our skill and guts. Can we find words to evoke love's bliss ("Grand to be alive, to be young / To be mad, to be yours alone"), its mischievous delights ("The way you wear your hat."), or its vain regrets ("Yesterday all my troubles seemed so far away."). Dare we reveal humiliating weakness ("Ever since you've been five years old / I've been a fool for you"), loneliness ("Blue moon, you saw me standing alone") or despair ("At break of dawn there is no sunrise / When your lover has gone."). Can we make our lyrics sigh, cry, moan, and whimper? Listen to this savage howl, edged with an ex-lover's vengeful gloating:

> I don't complain
> Through nights of endless pain,
> 'Cause I see your secret dreams,
> I hear your silent screams,
> I see the snake that eats your heart . . .

Heinrich Heine wrote that lyric (here translated by me) and Robert Schumann set it to music one hundred and fifty years ago. Let's top it if we can.

Dig deep into passion with your lyrics. Let your language get gauzily gorgeous if you please, but watch out for going gooily out of focus. True love has a certain stinging clarity. Don't be a prude, and, if you want, get raunchy—"Push, push in the bush" may be the most sexually explicit pop lyric I know—but I don't recommend it. How lyrics communicate is too mysterious a process for such literal-minded use. People prefer hearing "Ooh, baby, baby, let me love you all night long," and imagining the rest to you handing them a manual on how to insert Tab A into Slot B. The sexiest lyrics get steamy by suggestion. One chorus of "Teach Me Tonight" and we know this guy or gal isn't being taught trigonometry. "Should the teacher stand so near, my love? . . . Graduation's almost here, my love." Without a single off-color word, the lyric tells us this is a mating dance song, a man or woman coyly but eagerly surrendering to a night of delectable lovemaking. An old songwriting adage wisely declares, "Get 'em into bed by the bridge." Make sure your listeners know that your lovers love each other "all the way." Even if your song is about a gal *not* getting into bed with the guy she's crazy about, still let us know that's where she wants to be.

Never forget, however, that there's far more to love than romance. I urge you to let all kinds of love into your lyrics. Look back to the three cornerstones we laid down in the Introduction:

1. Love of Craft—You are writing lyrics because you love the art, the fun of writing and rewriting, even its ups and downs.
2. Love of Self—As Bob Dylan said, "Dig yourself." Don't get a swelled head, but believe in yourself and what you are saying.
3. Love of Other People—You are writing songs to talk with other people intimately in loving friendship.

Open your lyrics to all these loves and more. Love will guide you to new ideas, new insights, and new images. Love will refresh your tired wits, lead you past creative roadblocks, set your imagination afire.

I could go on and on, but then I'm a sucker for love and music. If you start singing a "silly love song"—"Oh my dear, our love is here to stay," "I love you a bushel and a peck, a bushel and a peck and a hug around the neck," "All you need is love, love, love is all you need"—I'll be right there singing with you, a happy grin on my face.

Here's a little story to show how love can sneak into our lyrics. In the summer of 1998, our wonderful nephew Joao-Paulo Fonseca, a brilliant, dashingly handsome twenty-six-year-old, newly married, starting out in life, was killed instantaneously in a car crash. Our whole grieving family gathered around his widow Jean and his parents, my sister Mary and her husband Wilton. After the funeral, Ellen and I came home to New York and tried to get back to work.

A few days later I found myself thinking, "JP's gone. What am I going to do with all the love I felt for him?" My student Dan was coming over that evening, and as I got out my guitar, I thought, "Dan is a nice young fellow like JP. I know, I'll pass the love I felt for JP on to Dan and other people in my life." As Dan and I worked, I could feel a current of love turning like a river in my heart, connecting me with Dan as it had connected me with JP. Soon, meeting friends old and new, I found myself saying inside, "Pass it on, Michael, pass it on," feeling each time the same strong turn in my heart. A month and more of mulling it all over and out came a lyric:

> When you get a little love, pass it on,
> You can give it all away, it's never gone,
> When someone's good to you, be good to someone new,
> 'Cause the only thing to do, when you get a little love, is
> Pass it on.

chapter 12

Refinements

By now I hope that chords and forms and lyrics and melodies and rhythms have become old friends of yours, well-loved tools that you can take out of your musical toolbox and—with some measuring, sawing, hammering, screwing, gluing, and head-scratching—use to construct songs that have, if not immortal beauty, at least a sturdy grace.

This means you're ready for the last lookover and the last edits, the sanding, polishing, and highlighting—the sparkling refinements that can turn a good song into a great one.

The trouble is that fiddling with a song past a certain point doesn't help. Even perfectionists have to know when to stop and say, "This song is done." So I've limited myself to three final refinements: *hooks*, *assonance*, and *the lovely flaw*.

Hooks

I hardly dare mention hooks because the word has been used so much and so loosely about pop songs—"Where's the hook?" "You gotta have a hook!"—that some hopefuls think writing songs is nothing more than writing hooks.

A hook is any song device, from an offbeat riff to a joking few words to a thundering repeated chorus, so well defined and well placed in the song that it leaps up from the musical flow and hooks the audience's attention. The drummer's "knock knock knock" in the pause as Ray Charles sings "I hear you knocking ... on my door" in "Hallelujah, I Just Love Her So," is a hook. The bass-voiced growl on The Miracles' "Love Machine" is a hook. So is George Harrison's guitar lick that opens "Day Tripper," and the stop-time rhythm that matches the lyric on The Supremes' "Stop! In the Name of Love." I think of

Hall and Oates hits like "Your Kiss is on My List" as songs filled with great hooks. Every four or eight-bar section seems to have a new vocal, lyrical, rhythmic, or instrumental twist that captures my interest. Listening, I keep feeling, "I love this part, oh, I love this new part even more," and soon I'm singing, tapping, and air-guitaring along. If people like a hook, they remember it, and they want to hear the song again so they can get hooked again. Hooks make hits, and that's why songwriters try to write hooks.

Look over your songs. Where are your hooks? Undoubtedly you have a few already. Your heart-phrase is undoubtedly your biggest hook. It states the big emotion you want listeners to understand and enjoy. You may already have come up with a catchy melody for the sing-a-long chorus or an exciting rhythm for the bridge.

Now is the time to ask, "Am I doing all I can to bring out those hooks, sharpen their edge, polish their gleam?" For example, "Love Machine's" basic hook is the funny, original heart-phrase, "I'm just a love machine, and I don't work on nobody but you." The song's driving rhythm matches the lyric, and the instrumental colors sound amusingly robotic. All of this is good, but then somebody had the bright idea, "I'll growl in a deep voice right *here*; it'll be the sound of the love machine." That final dab of cuteness is just what the other hooks need to bring them into focus and make the whole song stand out. Let's say you've got a new song, "You Got Me Cryin' Over You," that rocks into the chorus:

Example 129

That's a good hook, but if you add a little wah-wah cry like so:

Example 130 Track Seven

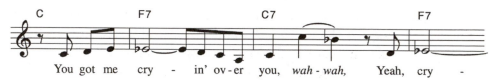

then you'll have added a mini-barb to the big hook that could spark everybody into singing along.

I love hooks, and I'm trying to write hooks myself, but I still caution you not to make hooks your be-all and end-all. Or better yet, don't think of hooks as something clamped onto your song to make it sell. The best hooks flow out of the music and lyrics naturally. They come to the listener's attention, not by saying, "I'm a hook, I'm a hook," but by distilling emotion into a few delightful sounds. "S'wonderful, s'marvelous" is one of the great hooks of all time, so suave, so charming that hear it once and you'll never forget it, you'll always be happy to hear it again. "S'wonderful, s'marvelous … " is not extra to the song, it *is* the song. Its soft curve perfectly captures the mood of a swooning lover.

Go and do likewise. As you set up the big flow of a song, keep its surface sparkling with distinct musical ideas. You can use almost anything—a shout, a laugh, an instrumental countermelody, a measure or two of stop-time—to punctuate the flow and give contrasting colors to succeeding song sections. Do this well, and listeners will hear hooks in your songs. At the same time remember that good hooks accent and highlight a song's big flow without obstructing it. Hooks that break the flow gotta go.

Assonance

Assonance, the music of similar word sounds, has come up already in discussing rhyme, alliteration, and sublime concoctions like "Chattanooga Choo Choo." Yet assonance is a subject broader even than these broad subsets, and I encourage you to go after all sorts of assonance in your lyrics.

Look at your latest lyric. You've got it in good shape. It says what you want to say. Now, can you make any small changes that will leave your meaning intact but make the word music more melodic, more memorable?

Start listening for assonance and you'll hear it everywhere. Repeated letters—"My g-g-g-g-generation."—and repeated word—"A kiss is still a kiss, a sigh is just a sigh"—create assonance. Puns are a form of assonance. We get a kick out of Chuck Berry's "Johnny B. Goode" because Johnny B. Goode is both the name of the guitar-playing hero and what we shout to encourage him rocking out: "Go, Johnny, go, Johnny be good." Listen for assonance and you'll soon hear *dissonance*, word sounds that sharply contrast. In my song, "Tell Me Lies," I love to sing this string of wah-wah sounds:

In this wide and weary world, what's one more broken heart …

but I'm also glad to get to the sharp *k* of "broken" that breaks the string.

Writing assonant lyrics can become a meticulous business. In her book, "How to Make a *Good* Song a *Hit* Song," songwriter Molly Ann Leikin describes how she rewrote "even so, I'm going away" to "even so, I'm leaving today" to get the "eve-leave" assonance. Years ago I struggled for weeks to get a line that would say, "smiles can conceal tears." "There are tears in every smile," was my first try. "Tears are inside every smile," was my second. Then I scratched and rescratched until I came up with "Tiny tears hide inside every smile," which gave me alliterative T's and a neat "hide-inside" interior rhyme. More recently, for my song, "Such A Tender Touch," I debated for days between:

The smile in your eyes says so much ...

or:

The smile in your eyes means so much ...

The first way I got the three initial *s*'s of "smile-says-so," but I finally chose the second, figuring that the two *m*'s of "means so much" mattered more.

At midnight when you're pacing your room and grinding your teeth in frustration, you'll think this is nitpicking. In saner moments you'll remember that going the distance for musical word sounds comes with the territory. The details we lyricists slave over listeners absorb semiconsciously at best, but the long life of lyrics by masters like Lorenz Hart, Hank Williams, and Bob Dylan prove that listeners recognize and love lyrics with an extra edge of musicality. Make the words as musical as the music. That's our goal, and getting there is well worth any blood, sweat, and tears we expend.

The Lovely Flaw

You've just written what feels like a great song, but when you play it through a few times, it sounds too perfect. The melody marches precisely up and down the scale, the chords follow each other with perfect logic, and the words tell the story clearly, but you have to admit, it's boring.

That's the time for the lovely flaw, a helpful expression I first heard from a songwriting pal. "Remember beauty spots," she asked, "the black dots that duchesses put on their cheeks in the time of Louis the XIV?" The duchesses believed these flaws in otherwise flawless complexions would draw eyes to their beauty, whereas bland perfection might be overlooked. Likewise, my pal argued, lovely musical flaws can draw ears to songs that, if perfect, might be underheard.

Look over any song that feels too good to be true. Where can you jog the melody out of its complacency, give a dissonant twist to the harmony, smudge the lyric with a gob of dirt to bring it back to earth? Can you flat any notes for an off-key, bluesy touch? Could a bump of syncopation knock a dull rhythm pleasingly off-kilter? Music has too many lovely flaw devices to list here, but two I like are:

- Break up a long passage of even 4/4 with a few measures of quarter-note triplets that, in effect, change the meter to 3/4:

Example 131 Track Seven

- Use an *appoggiatura*, or crushed note, a melody note not in the chord you're playing but which, after a beat or two, resolves to a chord tone. As an example of the latter: in writing my song, "Valentine Waltz," I first had the melody land on an E in fourth measure:

Example 132 Track Seven

Being the fifth of A, the E was consonant with the A7th chord playing beneath, but it sounded square to me. After trying this and that, I made the melody land on F and then resolved to E after a brief, poignant dissonance:

Example 133 Track Seven

Maybe your lyric needs a rough word, a rough rhyme, a more cutting conclusion. Paul McCartney started the song, "Getting Better," with its cheerful refrain, "It's getting better all the time," then John Lennon added the sour counter-refrain, "Can't get any worse." Is your lyric too grammatical? Schoolteachers frown on double negatives—"I don't want no lunch"—but songwriters love them—"Ain't no mountain high enough, ain't no valley low enough." Why? Because lovers speak without worrying about the rules of grammar. Your goal as a lyricist is not abstract, inhuman perfection but capturing the informal language spoken in your day. "There is not a thing you can accomplish" is a lousy lyric; "There ain't nothin' you can do" is a killer.

As we leave the art of songwriting and go on to its business, we leave our workrooms and step into the world. That's a giant step both inviting and daunting. Do we dare take it? Working in the world can make a good antidote to workroom loneliness, yet we are much more vulnerable in the world than behind the walls of our inner sanctum. They don't call it The School of Hard Knocks for nothing.

Do take the step. Music was not born to die in the workroom; music becomes music by being shared. Yes, you face tough competition from first-rate colleagues, and you face a world of people far too busy to stop and listen to you. Nights will come when you're ready to throw in the towel, when the weight of countless rejections will all but crush your spirit. Do retreat to the workroom to refresh your spirit, but don't give up. If you have something to say to the world in song, say it no matter what. Keep searching and you'll find opportunities. Take a just and steady pride in your work. Weaving words and music into songs, and singing and playing well enough to bring those songs to life, these are accomplishments worth a few sacrifices.

On those days when you feel knee-high to a very small grasshopper, dwarfed by faceless mega-corporations in tall glass towers, remember that we singer–songwriters are little guys with one big advantage: we can be wholly independent. Most everybody in the music business needs other people to keep their act together. Solo bass players, you'll notice, are few and far between. We songwriters who can accompany ourselves are modern one-man bands, capable of entertaining audiences and making records all by ourselves. Sure, in good times, we may hire a band and background singers, but if times turn bad, who needs 'em! Wandering minstrels are we, and whether we end up wearing silk suits or rags and patches, let's keep singing in the rain and sunny weather, wherever life takes us. "The best things in life are free," says a fine old song, and one of them is music.

part II

The Business of Songwriting

chapter 13

Business Basics

You've studied and written and played and sung and rewritten and rewritten some more. You have a fistful of songs and you're thinking, "Man, these sound pretty damn good."

Now what?

Now the hard part, getting anybody else on God's green earth to listen to them.

Selling songs can be discouraging work. You send demos out to hot prospects, and they get swallowed up by the Black Hole of Lost Demos. You plug a singer at a local club, and he says "No, man, the boss only wants me to sing songs everybody knows," or she says, "Sorry, hon, I only sing my own originals." You get out there and sing them yourself, and two ladies at a front table talk loudly about their cats. You make a CD and press a thousand copies. Fifty you give to pals and family, a hundred you send to record labels and publishers, and you sell ten a month at gigs. After a year you still have six hundred and forty-three left.

There's only one way to survive the struggle ahead: be a professional.

"Wait a second," you ask. "How can I be a professional when I've never sold a song?"

Easy. Being professional does mean trying to make money from your songs, but more basically, being professional is the attitude you take to your work. Thinking like a pro when you've got a nickel in your pocket and a million dreams in your heart, that's the way to turn that nickel into a dime and those dreams into dollars. Say to yourself right now, "From now on, I'm a professional songwriter." Stick to that commitment through hell or high water, and you'll be a pro.

What does being a pro involve? Many things, most of which you'll learn as you go along. Here I'll be summing up lessons I've learned since 1975 when a fan in Berkeley, California paid me $1 for the sheet music to my song "Cops and Robbers."

Starting a Business

Turning pro means turning your songwriting into a business, a company with goods and services to sell. It means committing yourself to a long-term, concerted effort to make money from your songs. You take the first steps in starting a business on your own, no lawyers or official papers needed.

The first three steps:

1. Think up a name for your company.
2. Buy a small ledger, available at any stationery shop.
3. In the ledger write the date, your company name, and a brief statement that you are starting a company to market your songs, then sign your name.

Take those three steps and you will have done much. Picking your company name can be fun. Go for a name that gives you an enjoyable kick. The date, declaration, and signature give you a founding moment: *You Music—Established 2004.* In the ledger, begin to record your business income and expenses, the first item being the cost of the ledger, a tax-deductible business expense. Now you've made your song-selling a defined aspect of your life, a business that will continue even when you take a vacation.

To thrive, every business needs elbow grease and brainpower. Stop by a Mom-and-Pop store in your neighborhood, and you'll soon see how much time and effort Mom and Pop put into maintaining and improving their business. Every day they mop the floors and every month they change the show-windows. They move fans up front in the summer and snow shovels up front in the winter. Long nighttimes after they close, Mom and Pop are still there checking inventory, paying bills, and talking over plans to expand. Your song store will require the same elbow grease and brain power from you. So far, you are the sole owner of this business. All decisions are yours to make; the buck stops with you.

I know: you're an artist, a genius writing songs the whole world will love, not a businessperson, a beancounter who sits at a desk all day in a suit and tie. Business is boring.

Ah, sweet illusions! Here's the nitty-gritty: To survive and succeed in the music business, you must become a knowledgeable music businessperson yourself. The music business has ins and outs that ordinary music lovers know nothing about. You've got a lot to learn, and now is the time for open-minded study. Drop any prejudices you may have about how greedy, corrupt, or anti-art the music business is; such snobberies are luxuries you cannot afford. Yes, there are crooks and bullies in the music business, and I'll show you how to protect yourself against them, but no matter what anybody else does, you can run your business as an honest endeavor. Be truthful in all your dealings, accurate to the penny in your accounts, and sell a product worth the price you're asking. An honest business person provides a valuable service to the world, becomes a reliable node in the vast network of people exchanging what they have for what they want. The money you earn from a song that people enjoy will pay for the dinner and a movie that you enjoy.

A follow-up step to the first three is ordering business cards and stationery printed with basic information: your company name, address, phone, fax, and e-mail. You may find you need a bank account separate from your personal account, a post office box address, a business phone and e-mail address, a web site. Later you may need a city or state business license, to incorporate and even trademark your company name, steps that will require a lawyer's help. Take these secondary steps slowly; you may not need much official paperwork for your first few years, and do not crush your little business with high startup costs.

Song Publishing

You write songs, so this business you're starting is a songwriting company, right?

Wrong, or at best, half right.

Yes, writing songs is your trade, and you can sell your songwriting services to others the way plumbers sell their plumbing services to customers, BUT (and this is important, so focus closely):

You'll put yourself in a much better business position if you consider that your core business is song publishing.

Here's why. In the music business, music publishers own the songs songwriters write, and they sell the rights to use them to record companies, singers, movie and television producers, advertising agencies, and the like. A songwriter can only launch a song in today's music marketplace through a publishing company that gives the writer and the song a commercial framework, a business home base.

Music publishers come in all sizes from tiny—Ellen's and my Mopat Music—to big—Cherry Hill Music—to humungous—Warner Bros. Music. Most have offices in New York, Nashville, or Los Angeles—the biggest in all three. Someday you may get hired by an established music publisher as a *contract writer* and write songs only for that company. Then you will be a songwriter pure and simple. For more about that career direction, see the *Contracts* chapter to come.

The chance, however, of you getting such a contract with a publisher when you are starting out is one in a million. For years, most likely, you'll be acting as your own publisher, producing and bankrolling your own demos, making the sales pitch phone calls, sending out the promo packages. Since you're going to have to think and act like a publisher, you might as well be one in earnest. How? By considering the company you've just started as a music publishing company owned by you.

Don't be afraid. Be proud. The big publishers in the glass towers may have the gold records and the Grammies, but they can't stop you from hanging out your shingle on Tin Pan Alley: "You Music—Quality Songs for Sale."

The music business offers a big incentive to publishing your own songs. The standard deal between songwriters and song publishers is a 50–50 split of all income. As your own publisher, therefore, you can keep 100 percent of the take, neatly doubling your earnings. Equally important, you'll be running your own show, making your own decisions. If you don't push a song, you'll have only yourself to blame. Some publishers have been known (horrors!) not to send songwriters every penny that's due them. When you are your own publisher, all the checks will come to you; whether you want to share them with your songwriter half, well, that's your business.

Be cautious, though; the picture isn't all that rosy. Signing with a big publisher can get your songs through doors closed to tiny independents. Fifty percent of a song pushed by Warner Bros. might well be worth more than one hundred percent of a song your company can't get anybody to listen to.

Still, thinking and acting as your own publisher is essential when you are starting out and will surely contribute to your long-term success. Remember that self-publishing can complement, not conflict with, signing with a major publisher. You may sign a contract but get dropped a year later. If you can't find a new deal, you'll have to self-publish to keep your career going. Your company may sign a *co-publishing deal* with a major publisher, getting the advantage of the big guy's clout but keeping a measure of your independence, and a piece at least of the publishing income. Quite possibly, after a dozen years, you will have some songs signed to one publisher, some with another, a few others co-published by yourself and a third company, and others still published solely by your company.

Taxes

One thing to look into right away is the valuable tax advantages of starting your own business. Confirm what follows with an accountant, but, in essence, under United States tax law a self-owned ("sole proprietor," in IRS language) business that earns income during the tax year can deduct all legitimate expenses paid out during that year to keep the business running. You do not need to earn a profit to deduct your expenses. For years, you may well run at a loss. All you need is some income from any aspect of your songwriting—performance fees, royalties, or commissions—and you can be a business in the eyes of the IRS.

Ask your accountant or the IRS for a *Schedule C*, the basic form for reporting income from a sole proprietorship. You'll see lines on which to report office, utility, travel, and car and truck expenses, as well "other expenses" lines where you'll fill in items specific to your songwriting business: studio and musician fees, music lessons, instruments, recording equipment, and more. If you set aside a room in your house, even a corner of your apartment, to be your business office, you may be able to deduct a portion of your rent or mortgage as a legitimate expense.

Don't pad your expenses—you'll risk a highly unpleasant audit that could lead to substantial fines and penalties—but do use your ledger to note every dime you spend to advance your business. If you buy a CD to give to your Dad for Christmas, that's not a business expense. If you buy the same CD so you can study the artist's style and figure out what songs to send him or her, that is a business expense.

Copyright

Article I, section 8 of the United States constitution grants Congress the power "to promote the progress of science and the useful arts by securing for limited times to authors and inventors the exclusive right to their respective writings and discoveries."

This is the basis for all American copyright law; copyright covers all forms of songwriting, music and words. What Article I section 8 means for you is that you own the right to copy what you write because you wrote it. No one else has permission to copy, use, or sell your work unless you make an agreement to give, rent, or sell them the right to do so. Through the 20th century Congress steadily lengthened the "limited times" of the Constitution. The current copyright term lasts the lifetime of the author plus seventy-five years. That's a long time through which your songs could earn you and your heirs a lot of money. You must therefore learn right away how to secure the copyright to your songs.

The first step is to write the international copyright symbol ($©$), your name, and the year you competed the song on the finished lead sheet of all your songs, like so:

© John Doe 2004

Make sure that this copyright notice gets on every photocopy you make of your songs. Also, put it on the cases of all CDs and cassettes you send out as well as on the CDs and cassettes themselves.

You do not need to register the copyright of every song you write the minute you write it, but do get in touch right away with:

Register of Copyrights
Library of Congress
Washington, D.C. 20559
202-707-3000
www.copyright.gov

The Register of Copyrights will gladly send you forms and pamphlets to help you register the copyright of your songs when you need to. When is that? When commercial activity starts on one of your songs: if you record it for public release or if you get serious interest from an artist or producer. Currently it costs $30 to copyright a song, but you can save money by registering several songs on one form, calling them "Songs of Spring 2004," for example.

Dozens of songwriting legends tell about the down-on-his-luck songwriter who sold a song copyright for $50 and a bottle of whisky, only to see the lucky buyer make it a smash hit, leaving the songwriter broke and singing the blues. This sad story is not as likely as legend suggests, but do not let it happen to you. An old saying in all creative art business is "NEVER sell your copyrights." This is excellent advice. Many songwriters, we'll soon see, sign contracts with publishers who then own the copyrights to the songs written under the contract, but such contracts specify royalty payments based on a percentage of the song's income. At the right time and place, that can be a good decision. But please, never sell a song copyright for a one-time, lump-sum payment.

ASCAP, BMI, and SESAC

Though you don't need to join immediately, you do need now to find out about the *performing rights societies*. There are the two giants: American Society of Composers, Authors, and Publishers (ASCAP), and Broadcast Music Inc. (BMI). The Society of European State Authors and Composers (SESAC) is a smaller but still important performing rights group, largely in church music. The Appendix lists their addresses and web sites. All three will be glad to send you information about their procedures and the advantages each has over the other two. You can belong to a performing rights group as a songwriter and as a publisher; Ellen and I and Mopat Music belong to ASCAP.

What ASCAP, BMI, and SESAC do, in essence, is license their members' songs for performance on radio and television, in restaurants and nightclubs. After paying the licensing fees, music users are free to play any song in the society's huge catalogs. The societies randomly sample radio airplay, TV show logs, and other performance outlets, then wield complex formulas to divide the licensing fees fairly among their members. For hit songwriters, performing rights income can become astronomical, and even middle-level writers can earn a pleasant flow of checks that come in, rain or shine, every three months.

When can you join a performing rights society? As soon as you get your first songwriting deal. That can include you recording your own songs and putting them out your own CD, an excellent idea, by the way, which we'll discuss further in *Getting Heard*. Both ASCAP and BMI—SESAC is not for pop song beginners—accept a professionally produced CD as proof that your songs are launched in the music marketplace and that you and your company are worthy of their licensing protection.

Belonging to ASCAP and BMI will cost you modest dues, but you'll find your money well spent from the start. Both societies have helpful staff, and problems that may baffle you are old hat to them. Society newsletters will keep you abreast of what's happening in the biz and list programs, seminars, and grants designed to encourage, educate, and reward new members. BMI's Lehman Engel Music Theater Workshop, for example, has nurtured many up-and-coming Broadway songwriters.

Join ASCAP or BMI as soon as you can, and you'll gain a valuable ally in the struggles that lie ahead. Use your membership actively and wisely, and you'll find opportunities and earnings you never could find on your own.

Business Plans and Goals

Every book about starting a business tells its readers to *have a plan* and to *set goals*. I'm not about to break the mold. "Have a plan" and "Set goals" may be clichés, but they're true.

In the first few months of your business, spend time mulling over what you're doing. What do you hope to accomplish? How do you hope to accomplish it? Write your answers down. Think of the rewards and pleasures you long for, the losses or pains you fear. Write these pluses and minuses down too. Let it lie a few days then look again and change anything you've thought twice about. Do that a few times and soon a core of methods and goals will emerge from inside you. Instead of darting here and there on impulse, you'll have a defined plan of action that mixes high and low-priority goals, that details what you're going to do this week, and sketches where you hope to be five years from now. This is your business plan. It will grow and change, but if you take your time creating it, you'll be surprised how long your plan will last.

Set artistic and financial targets you hope to hit. No need to declare hard-and-fast deadlines by which you must reach your goals or give up, but review your progress every month, six months, and year. If you find you're reaching your goals, great, then it's time to set new ones. If you find you're falling short, analyze why. Maybe you've set goals unrealistically high; maybe you're forgetting a crucial factor. Whatever the results, use them to modify your strategies.

Plans and goals can help protect you against discouragement in an emotionally topsy-turvy business. For example, some years ago I hoped to launch Mike and the Lytones, a five-piece band—electric keyboard and guitar, tenor sax, bass, and drums—playing pop-jazz originals and standards. A few similar projects had crashed and burned, casting me down for months. This time, I decided, I'll make a plan. I'll find players, rehearse, make a four-song demo, and line up five neighborhood gigs. At the end of two months, I'd review whether to stop or go on. I decided to stop, as it turned out, but found myself not crying my usual band-went-nowhere blues. The pride I took in running a controlled experiment outweighed my disappointment.

Investment

Your ledger will cost you a few bucks. Your business cards, stationery, manuscript paper, and phone calls will cost a few more bucks. Your studio time, musician fees, and demo duping will cost you a lot more bucks. Where are all those bucks going to come from? What chance is there that someday, somehow, an inflow of earnings will ever reverse the endless outflow of expenses?

Even millionaires don't like throwing good money after bad. For the rest of us on limited budgets, spending and spending and getting no return can be, at first, dispiriting and then terrifying. Yet face the fact that *your startup business will need investment.* This is a nice way of saying that, for years, you'll be spending money with no guarantee that you'll ever see it again.

To calm your fears, here are a few comforting thoughts. You're not alone. Every business from the biggest to the smallest needs investment to "prime the pump," as economists say. Ford has to build a car before they can sell it, and Mom and Pop had to pay first and last months' rent on their shop before they could sell a single candy bar. Songwriting is, comparatively, a low-investment business. There are no factories to construct, no raw materials to buy, no salaries to pay. Watch your pennies, and a thousand dollars will go a long way. Keep your ledger and keep reviewing your business plan, and you'll know where the money is going and why. This is a better feeling than watching helplessly as your life savings sluice uncontrollably down the drain.

I don't know how much you can afford to invest in your songwriting business, or how much help you can get from family, friends, a credit union or bank, so going into dollar amounts would make no sense. Here are three general tips:

- Spend slowly. Investment involves time as well as money. X dollars spent over six months is much easier on the pocketbook than X dollars spent in a week. If you devote April to recording a high cost demo, devote May and June to selling the demo with low-cost phone calls, packaging, and postage.
- Spend wisely. Maybe your computer doesn't need every bell and whistle. Take a bus, not a cab. Go home after a gig instead of spending half your pay on drinks with the gang. You don't need to express mail every promo pack; first class will do just fine for all but a few. What you save by cutting down wasteful spending will still be in the bank when you want it.
- Avoid debt. Fund your investments from your overall flow of income, even if that means staying with a day job that bores you to tears. Carrying large credit card balances from month to month is a wasteful habit. Keep any bank or personal loans you arrange as small as possible, and reduce or retire them before you borrow again. Bringing in outside money may diminish your ownership of your company; many fledgling entrepreneurs have seen their companies slip away to creditors they could not pay.

Work through the steps outlined above, taking each step at your own pace, and I guarantee that in time you'll get a grip on the basics of the songwriting business. By a slow accumulation of knowledge and experience, you will begin to feel like, and in fact be, a professional songwriter—maybe still an apprentice with much to learn, but no longer a disorganized and naive amateur. Will you have made any money? Maybe, maybe not, but you will have set up the channels through which future money could flow. You will also have joined an illustrious band of songwriter–publishers—Irving Berlin heading the list, Curtis Mayfield and Bob Dylan not far behind—who have taken their independent way in the music marketplace, matching their musical skills with their commercial savvy, making a good living making good music.

chapter 14

Getting Heard

Performing

The quickest, simplest, and cheapest way to start getting your songs heard in the world is to play and sing them in public yourself. Perform, perform, perform!

Fortunately, since the 1960s, "singer–songwriter" has become a distinct music business niche. Many intimate clubs specialize in booking singer–songwriters, and many listeners enjoy hearing their personal, independent voices. Audiences (and cost-conscious producers) like the simplicity of a singer–songwriter act: one person, one instrument, one mike. This means that you have no excuse not to get out there. Put together a band if you can, but do not wait for a band. Get some solo time under your belt to develop your persona, to prove that you can stand on your "one human singing and playing" foundation.

As we saw chapters ago, nearly every community in America offers you places to perform. Your job now is to find and go to them, introduce yourself, and say you'd like to play there. Ask who books the musicians and what you'll need to do to audition. That first trip will be your gig-hunting debut. Congratulations! Stay in the business and you'll never stop.

If you get a gig (by this I mean any scheduled performance; you'll play plenty of worthwhile gigs for no pay), you'll rehearse what you plan to play and get to the venue in plenty of time. You'll interact courteously with everyone who's working with you. You'll perform to the very best of your ability. You'll bow, say "thanks" and "good night" to all concerned, and leave.

I say you'll do this because, if you don't act this professionally on your gigs, you won't be in the business long. The celebrity press tells us about stadium-filling stars who wreck dressing rooms in drunken tantrums. Until you're filling stadiums, and even then, I don't recommend it. Being polite, together, and on time is taken for granted as a minimum standard of behavior among working musicians. No one expects you to be perfect—"Everybody plays the fool sometimes," says a great song—but be forewarned that bookers, agents, stagehands, bartenders, and your fellow musicians don't like rude, late, know-it-all jerks.

Whenever you appear in public as a professional, at a club, radio station or record company office, you're a walking advertisement for yourself. Dress well according to your own taste. Be willing to meet people, say hello with a smile. Tell people about yourself with confidence, ask them about what they do with interest. Give them your card, ask for theirs. Since you're a performer, people will expect you to be an outgoing personality. Unless you overdo it, they won't mind if you talk yourself up or give them a cassette, publicity flyer, or promo kit. *Polite persistence*, that's the rule of salesmanship, and now you're a salesman for yourself.

As your gigs increase and your price goes up, you may want to invest more in your act: newspaper ads, back-up musicians, your own PA system, a van, a video… and on and on. As I said before, go slowly. No one expects fog machines and dancing girls from a singer–songwriter, and a professionally produced video will not make you a star overnight. A clean little PA that you can carry is much better than a stadium-shaker that breaks your back. You can turn out a neat promo kit on your computer; the old-fashioned 8-by-10 black and white glossy photo is still a basic item in every performer's sales kit.

Recording

For most songwriters, getting their songs recorded is the biggest goal of all: "Somebody, *anybody*, please put my song on wax." Earnings are a big factor, of course, because only recorded songs make money in the marketplace, but yearnings count too. Once recorded, a song becomes *real*, no longer an air blown in on one breeze, blown out on the next, but a work of art captured in a lasting medium. A song on record, like the nymph on John Keats' Grecian urn, is a thing of beauty and a joy forever.

Utterly nonexistent a century and a half ago, sound recording grew up with movie film, and their histories are similar. Both began by taking snapshots of reality—a microphone capturing a baby's cries, a camera capturing the look of his teary face—and both have grown into sophisticated media that create their own reality. Records today spin highly artificial webs of sound from dozens of tracks and dozens of sources, electric or acoustic, human or computer-generated. Recording has become a vital branch of modern music, and being creative in the studio takes study as disciplined as the study you're lavishing on your writing, your instrument, and your voice.

Though painstaking compared to go-with-the-flow performing, recording has its own exhilarating pleasures. Hearing your voice booming out of big speakers, so clear, so present, so cushioned on smoothly interwoven instruments—that's an unbeatable thrill. The only snag about recording is that it's expensive. Performing earns money and needs only a trickle of expenses to support. Recording means a clock ticking at $50, $60, or $100 or more an hour with you paying the tab. "Getting a few songs down," you think, "how long could it take?" But with that frog in your throat here, forgetting a lyric there, then the mixing, the editing, and those overdubs you've got to have, a half-dozen hours have flown by, and you're not half done.

The variety of options that modern recording techniques offer can bewilder the beginner: live instruments or sampled instruments, sixteen or thirty-two track, concert hall reverb or small room reverb, to compress or not to compress? Most of these questions you'll answer on your own, depending on your taste, your budget, the song, and whether you want to experiment or imitate. Here let's discuss three big questions: *Home studio or pro studio? Demo or master? Who pays the costs?*

Home or pro? The big plus of recording in a home studio is independence. No clock, no engineer set in his ways, no next client waiting impatiently in the control booth. A second plus, over time, is cost. A well-designed home setup may last you so long that, averaged out, you'll be paying only a few dollars an hour to record. Short term, however, home recording has the minus of high startup costs. A good home studio will cost in the high four figures and quite likely spill into five figures. You may soon find you need expensive upgrades and updates.

Working in a pro studio has the plus that, if you make use of every minute, you'll pay a slow flow of medium-level costs. You will pay more in the long run, perhaps, than you'd pay for a home studio but spread out so that each month you can read your credit card bill without fainting. A second plus of a pro studio for some songwriters (me included) is that we don't like going past a certain point in sound technology. I like working with a good engineer and gladly let him set mike levels, plug and unplug mysterious wires, work magic with the EQ pots. I may say a lot over his shoulder, and he'll sometimes let me nudge a fader up or down, but my job is making good music. The engineer has his job, making that music sound good on record. Unless you love digging into the nitty-gritty of electronics, I recommend working in pro studios.

The home or pro studio question relates to the demo or master question. Demos are suggestive sketches for industry ears only, sneak peeks that say: "Hear how good this song sounds? Imagine how much better it's going to sound when your artist sings it with an orchestra." A finished master recording is the song polished for public ears, with all the voices and instruments and colors that you dreamed of, damn the expense.

For demos, a home studio or the little sixteen-track room around the corner will do just fine, and you can record solo. Simple solo demos have sold many a good song. If you want to enrich your sound, bass, drums, and a horn plus your own piano, synth, or guitar will be all the instruments you'll need. Don't book the highest-priced studio cats in town. A few reliable buddies will do a good job for you. Sing yourself unless the song does not suit you. If you book a singer, then you sing the back-up harmony. Mix and edit efficiently. Don't get finicky about minor details.

Making a master recording is a whole different ballgame. Now you may need the hotshot digital room downtown that has every sound-bending device known to man, a producer as well as an engineer, a singer who's making a noise in your neck of the woods, and a harmony vocal team with lots of jingle experience on their resume. You'll need studio cats who know their stuff, horns and/or strings, and an arranger to write their charts. After you've got everything in the can, you face weeks of mixing, remixing, and remixing some more. You'll need all this except—and this is a big except—at those times when demo-like simplicity is what the song requires. Then, just as for a demo, all you'll need is a few mikes, a few pals, and the right spirit.

Start with demos, the immediate tool you need to launch your song selling. Record solo or duo. You've got a lot to learn about recording, and floundering on your own is both less expensive and less embarrassing than floundering before a room full of cats waiting for you to tell them what to do. As you get more studio time under your belt and learn recording's curious rhythms and demands, you can build out from your foundation, bring in new musicians, try sound-shaping experiments, and start thinking of going on to a master recording you could release.

Who pays for your demos? The short answer is that you do, certainly at first. You'll pay for demos you make to get publishers interested in your work. Then with time and increasing success, you can start shifting demo costs to the publisher. Here's a possible scenario. You make a guitar, bass, and drums demo that costs you $300. Joe at Mega Music likes it but tells you that he needs a more finished recording to shop the song and that he wants you to redo the demo. "Fine," you say. "But Mega Music will have to put up some money." Joe reluctantly agrees to pay half the new demo's costs but insists on charging that amount against your royalties. Eager to get started, you agree and make the demo. Joe sells the song, and lo and behold, it's a hit. When you offer Joe your next song, you've got more clout. You ask Mega Music to reimburse half your original demo costs and to pay all the costs of the second demo, charging only half of what they outlay against your royalty. You get some but not all of what you ask for. If the second song becomes a second hit, you'll get a still better deal on demo costs for the third song you sell.

However you record, home or pro, demo or master, and no matter who pays the bills, *keep control over your recording costs*. Ask yourself two questions before every session: How much can I afford? How much do I hope to earn? Whatever you answer, and answer conservatively, don't go beyond those limits. If Mega Music is underwriting the demo, Joe will be impressed and delighted if you bring a project in under budget. Extra bucks out will not guarantee extra bucks in. Sometimes the simplest recording tickles the public most. Paul McCartney's solo "Blackbird" at the end of the Beatles' complex *White Album* may be the album's best-loved track.

Three overall tips about recording:

- Be prepared. Ad-libbing on stage can often be a creative joy; ad-libbing in the studio is nearly always an expensive disaster. Know the songs you're going to record, the order you want to record them in, and the order you plan to lay down your tracks: rhythm section, then voice, horns, and overdubs is standard. Rehearse your part and any solos or set licks weeks in advance. Stick to your game plan through a session. If the plan isn't working, don't leap desperately into unplanned turmoil. Stop, take the tapes home, listen, analyze, and go back to a fresh session with a fresh plan. Prepare, prepare, prepare; you'll do better work for less money
- Shade the style of your demos to the market you want to reach. When actors audition for a part, they don't wear full costume, but they do let their outfits suggest the role: jeans and a bandanna for a cowboy, suit and tie for a lawyer. Do likewise with your demos. For a folk song, use guitar and bass; for a Broadway song, use piano and bass; for a rock song, use electric guitar, keyboard, bass, and drums. If you think your latest song could hit in Nashville, a spot of sweet pedal steel guitar will point your listeners in that direction. When you send a jazz singer the same song, drop the pedal steel and overdub a growling tenor sax.
- Most importantly, make every recording session a challenging, interesting experience. Whether you are alone with your piano or surrounded by a string orchestra, three oboes, two synthesizer wizards, and a conga player, *make every recording as good as you possibly can*. Accept your budgetary

limits. Find ways to be creative within them. Learn, learn, learn. Try to keep some recording activity going even through dry spells so your skill and your ears don't get dull. As a singer–songwriter, recording is now part of your work and your life. Enjoy it.

 Track 7 gives an example of a guitar–voice demo. Track 8 is an example of a fully produced demo.

Selling Your Songs

You'll be selling your songs every time you perform, send out a promo kit, or give a business card to a gal you meet while you both cool your heels in a bigwig's waiting room. There's no telling in the music business what a chance encounter may lead to. Maybe not to the Big Break we all dream about, but hopefully to the daisy chain of little breaks we all live on: a gig at the Cool Club leading to a gig at the Hot Club, an artist you meet introducing you to her producer who introduces you to a label executive. *Networking*, that's the modern name for the process, and network we must. Being a wallflower won't sell songs; you've got to get out there and mingle with your colleagues.

You'll also go on concerted campaigns to sell certain songs to certain artists, producers, A&R men, and established publishers. This week-in-week-out selling will be the meat of your work as a songwriter–publisher. Create an office routine to handle it: alphabetical files of lyrics and lead sheets by your desk, a basic sales letter in your computer that you'll adapt as necessary, a bio, gig flyers and photocopied reviews, as well as stationery, envelopes, a postage scale, fax machine, a good cassette duper and/or a CD-burning computer. With your office in place, you're ready to start calling possible targets. Yes, you will get hung up on, put on hold for eternity, and told, "I'm sorry, Mr. Smith (Jones Miller Williams) is out to lunch (in conference on the Coast in Europe). Keep smiling and keep calling—polite persistence, remember? One day you will get through to Bob at Hotshot Records, and he'll say, "OK, OK, send me a tape." Boom, you can have a demo kit in the mail to him five minutes after you hang up.

Make your demo kit an attractive package: clean graphics, typo-free typing, the demo neatly labeled with the titles, copyright notice, your name and phone, fax, and your e-mail and postal addresses. A typical kit will contain:

1. A demo of three to five songs, no more.
2. A business letter plugging the song and introducing yourself.

3. Typed lyric sheets for the songs; lead sheets if requested.
4. A recent flyer or press clipping.

Who will you send your demo kits to? The rule, obvious but worth remembering, is: *Look for likes*. Seek out performers and companies you already admire, whose work is something like yours. If you're writing country songs, go after country singers and publishers. If you're writing Latin songs, gospel songs, or rock songs, go where that action is. Being realistic about where you and your material fits in will save you charging up dozens of dead ends. Someday you may be a crossover superstar. Now, be happy to find your niche and expand inside it.

Send your kits to *people*, not companies. A kit addressed to "A&R Department Sony Records" will get buried in the slush pile. If at all possible, get a name, and have spoken to the person behind the name, before you send a kit. Find out what procedure your target likes to follow for reviewing demos. Remember that she may be getting dozens of kits every day. Unless invited, don't sent demo kits to more successful songwriters. You may love their work, but in their eyes now you are a competitor, not a fan. Many successful songwriters won't listen to unsolicited songs, sensibly protecting themselves from "You copied my song" lawsuits cropping up years later.

Start locally. Within a hundred miles of your hometown are sure to be a few club circuits, small labels, television producers, and ad agencies. Make your first calls to the performers playing these circuits, the people behind these businesses. They'll be a lot easier to get in to see than an Arista A&R man, and since they're nearby, you'll be able to build long-term relationships with drop-in visits. Exploratory trips to the music business' three hubs, New York, Nashville, and Los Angeles, can be a good idea. You'll surely send demos to many of their zip codes, and one day you may move to a hub. Still, don't neglect your home turf. An LA publisher will be more interested in someone already making a noise in Dallas than an unknown voice on the phone from Nagodoches, Texas.

Selling ain't always fun. Your targets may be indifferent, downright rude, or, what's worse, effusively friendly one day and icily distant the next. Many times your hopes will be dashed, done deals will come undone, hot prospects will turn cool. The best defense against such disappointments is to *sell to as wide a circle as you can*. Don't pin all your hopes on one or two prospects. Instead, send the same demo to five prospects at once. Remember that rejections feel personal but seldom are. "No thanks," from Louise at Alpha Music doesn't mean that your song is bad and that you're a bum. It means the chemistry wasn't right that time. Maybe you'll click with Louise on your next song, or with Tom at Omega Music on the first one. Great artists get the most rejections, an old Broadway saying goes, because great artists never stop trying.

If a target says no, let them off the hook. Don't beg, guilt-trip, or yell at anybody you're selling to. No one is required to record your songs or to explain why they don't want to. Deciding to record a song is a matter of taste. Do you like a salesman hanging over you, pushing you toward a product that you know you don't want? I didn't think so. When an artist, producer, or A&R man passes on a song, business etiquette requires you to respond, "Well, too bad, but thanks for considering it. I'll try you again when I have something that might suit you better." As my partner Ellen Mandel put it in a great lyric, "Smile when you say goodbye, you may want to come back."

Let's say goodbye to song selling for the moment with two minor questions and one big tip. The first minor question is that with each kit costing $10 or more, you'll often wonder, "Is this target worth the money?" That can be a tough call. If two demos to the same target disappear into the void, think hard about sending a third. My basic advice, though, is: Don't hoard your demos. A demo can do you more good out in the world than on a shelf in your closet. The second minor question is, "Do you put the name of your publishing company on a demo you're sending to a publishing company?" Sometimes yes, sometimes no—to a small company that might make a co-publishing deal, maybe; to a major publisher where you'd love to get signed up as a contract writer, probably not.

The big tip: *follow-up*. One phone call and a demo kit won't do the trick. Two phone calls and two demo kits won't do the trick. What sells songs, what sells anything, is follow-up, the series of contacts that creates an ongoing, enjoyable, and trustworthy relationship between buyer and seller. Your targets are people like you, men and women with families, friends, and hobbies they go home to. As you sell, find ways to make personal contact with your buyers, to get to know them and let them know you. Suggest lunch or a cup of coffee. Answer their calls and e-mails promptly. If you haven't heard from a prospect in a month or two, call and leave a "Hi, what's up?" message on their machine. You want to be someone people in the business are glad to hear from even when there's no business to do. The day will come when there's business to be done, and then you, the familiar face, will get the nod over the unknown newcomer.

Publicity

Unknown... That's what you're trying not to be. To become known by the business and the public, you need *publicity*.

Show business publicity pervades modern life; we take it in with the air we breathe. We follow celebrities and their star-spangled lives, this one rising, that one sinking, this one getting married, that one getting divorced. We read their profiles in glossy magazines and watch them on the Oscars and Emmys and Tonys and music awards shows. We read reviews to know which of their movies to go to, which of their CDs to buy. We fall asleep watching stars plugging new projects on the late-night talk shows, and we wake up to see the same stars plugging the same projects on the morning talk shows.

Year after year this gaudy parade passes by, and we seldom realize that it's all publicity, a gigantic multimedia machine maintained by experts well-paid to launch stars, start fashions, and titillate the public. Why is publicity so vital to show business? Because publicity sells show business products: actors, movies, TV shows, videos, CDs, action figures, and of course, singers and songs. Obvious, you say, "How can people buy something if they don't know about it?" True, but the power of publicity goes far beyond providing neutral information.

Publicity works magic on the human spirit, magic that a little introspection can measure. Think of a well-known star you like, then think of a friend known only to your circle. Do you put the star and the friend in separate mental categories? You know your friend better than the star, but you may feel you know and love the star. If you met your star in the flesh, that would be a Big Day in your life. If your friend became a star, wouldn't you be amazed, even jealous? What if you became a star? Wow, what would that feel like? Would it change how you and your friend feel about each other? "Never," you say, but think again. "I try to be friends with my old pals," many new stars report honestly, "but they treat me differently now." The subtle sense, enjoyable but slightly queasy, that stars are people set apart from the rest of us by an aura of fame and talent and success, that is *star power.* Few are born with star power; most pros achieve it by patient years working on their publicity.

You need to put publicity's magic to work for you, to sprinkle a little stardust on yourself and your songs. Publicity's mechanics are the same as selling. Keep a stream of phone calls, faxes, e-mails, and promo kits going out to any and all available publicity outlets: listings editors, newspaper reviewers and feature writers, DJs and club owners, radio and TV talk show producers. Think up a giveaway gimmick, a button or bumper sticker imprinted with your name and a catchy slogan. Play benefits and similar gigs that put you in front of a good audience for free—but don't think the dispiriting thought, "I'm not getting paid," think, "I'm investing my time for valuable publicity."

Give every send-out a *publicity angle.* For feature writers, "Songwriter Joe Smith will be at Benny's Club this Friday at 8" is a listing, not a story. There is the core of a story in:

Singer–songwriter Joe Smith is making his debut at Benny's
Friday ...

or

Satirical songwriter Joe Smith will be playing his new song about
the President at Benny's ...

or

Balladeer Joe Smith will be swinging and swaying lovers at
Benny's ...

All of these have the two essential ingredients of a publicity plug: *a name*
and *an angle*. To get noticed in the battle for column inches and screen time,
you need to get your name plus a brief identifying angle before the public. Find
your angle in your persona. Write up a one-page bio that tells your life story;
include big facts like where you were born, when you started playing, and a
few oddball, revealing details: "I like pizza with onions." Boil that down to a
slogan like, "Jazz and blues from a gal who's paid her dues," or a fanciful name,
like the "Cosmic Cowboy from Kentucky."

Let Tom Waits inspire you as a songwriter who has created a consistent
publicity image based on a unique persona. Whether you like Tom Waits or
not, you know he's the singer–songwriter who sleeps in his car. His scratchy
voice and deadpan lyrics, his funky, old-fashioned bands, and the Skid Row
locales of his album covers all contribute to one name and angle: Tom Waits,
poet of the down-and-out. Waylon Jennings and Merle Haggard were singer–
songwriters lost in the Nashville shuffle until somebody came up with the tag,
The Outlaws, a rebellious image that set them apart from the pack. You need
to develop an image that suits you from your life story and your music. How
do you want the public to see you? That's the big question; answer it by doing
everything you can to define a public image you want, one that gives you both
a framework and the freedom to be yourself.

Start your publicity efforts locally. Stardom, fortunately, comes in an
infinite number of degrees. If you've got the regular Thursday night slot at
Benny's, you're a star to the hopefuls who come to Wednesday's open mike;
you in turn are hoping to shine among the superstars who play the joint on
the weekends. You'll climb your local stardom ladder by steadily improving
your music, but I can tell you from experience that you may practice all day
and see your audience half-fill the club week after week, then one radio
interview with a popular disc jockey, and when you get to the club, there'll
be a line outside the door.

Advertising is publicity you pay for. Except for occasional small ads to plug club gigs, I do not recommend it. Few songwriters starting out can afford an ad campaign big enough to increase earnings, and in any case, the free publicity of interviews and reviews is more effective. People tend to believe, rightly or wrongly, that news columns report impartial facts and that ads hype half-truths.

To the old question, "Which is better, good publicity or bad publicity?" some old pros answer, "Good or bad, it's all publicity." That's not untrue. Big careers have been made by singer–songwriters who smash up hotel rooms and bare their unhappy private lives in confessional interviews. But as a beginner, protect your fledgling reputation. Being known as a hardworking, straight-shooting, and straight-talking pro—that's your best bet for success.

If you get interviewed, *be positive*. Don't say negative things about yourself. "Gotta admit, things have been slow lately," sounds weaker than, "I've got time now to work on my own projects." Avoid getting drawn into saying negative things about other people, particularly other singer–songwriters. It's a quick way to make an enemy (and they will hear about it—bad news travels fast), and the public as a rule doesn't like badmouthing. No need to lie, but you can back off from criticizing a colleague by saying something bland like, "I don't know her music well," or, "He's not one of my favorites, but that's just my taste. I know a lot of people like him."

Follow-up matters as much in publicity as in selling. Send thank you notes to your press contacts when they give you a plug, drop them an appreciative word when you read a piece of theirs you like. Make one publicity break lead to another; a local TV station will be more likely to book you on their "Arts at Noon" show if you've already done a few community access cable gigs. Clip out your good reviews and features, photocopy them, and send them to your whole network. You may discover something that amazed me the first time it happened: People will not remember you sent the clipping to them, and the next time you see them, they'll say, "Oh, I saw your picture in the *Chronicle*."

As you get more publicity, people in and out of the business will see you differently. One wonderful day someone will stop you on the street and say, "Oh, I know you, I saw your picture in the paper." You'll walk into a club and notice a new respect from the bartender and the sound man. Enjoy your growing stardom and the opportunities it creates for you and your songs, but don't get a swelled head. You're still silly old you, after all. You put your pants on one leg at a time like you always did. Keep your press releases perky but honest, and keep sending them out, but remember: Don't believe every word they say—it's all publicity.

Your Own Record Company?

I'm putting this last with a question mark because starting your own label, though not a bad idea, may be a bridge too far for most beginners.

Let's say you've had a bit of success, got some dough in your pocket and a good little band. You get a dozen tunes down in the studio, and they sound good. You shop it to a few labels, but they pass. What are you going to do? With a good computer, you burn thirty CDs, make a snazzy cover and label, and start selling them at gigs. The thirty sell out; so do a second thirty. Then you find a good company that'll press you a thousand copies for a decent prices, barcode thrown in for free. But as songs need publishers to survive in the music marketplace, records need record companies. To release your masterpiece, you need to found a record label. Again, get a ledger and write the company's name and purpose, sign it with the date, and, *voila*, a brand new indie is born.

Starting a label can be a smart move. Given today's technology, manufacturing CDs requires only low to moderate investment. Unlike giveaway demos, sold records may finally pay back your recording costs. Having a released album, shrink-wrap and all, will boost your prestige on your club circuit. You don't have to tell everyone that BingBong Records is you and you alone. The lessons you learn producing and selling your own record will stand you in good stead when you negotiate with a "real" label. If you're game, I encourage you to try starting a label. Ellen and I founded Brite Records in the 1980s to release our debut 45. Since then we've released four CDs. You may do well, even gather other artists around you until you have a small but still "real" label of your own.

Yet adding a label to your other efforts might take time and energy you'd rather give to music. A label's expenses, though low, are still considerable. Most songwriters who do press a thousand copies find that they sell slowly. Indies centered on one artist have a hard time finding a distributor, and without a distributor you can't get your CD into most stores. Review copies sent to likely magazines disappear just like your demos.

So think twice before starting a label. Remember how deciding the home-studio/pro-studio question depended partly on how much you do or don't love wires? To start or not to start a label can be put to a similar test: How much do you love paper and paper clips, trips to the post office, and making sales calls? You're already doing a lot of office work. Do you want to add another thirty percent? If you don't, look for someone who does. Maybe you'll be able to gather around his or her label, sharing expenses and work time, but not running the office every day yourself.

chapter 15

Song Contracts

One day the phone will ring. "Oh no," you'll think as you pick up the phone, "It's the garage, my car does need a new radiator." Instead, a strange voice will say words you've been hoping to hear ever since you strummed your first chord:

"Hello, are you the writer who sent us 'Shake It, Sexy Lady'? Well, we love it, just the song for our artist, Steve Superstar. Let's make a deal."

After you pick yourself up from the floor, I hope you'll be able, first, to stammer out a few words indicating how happy you are to get the call, and second, to get off the phone without making any definite commitment. At this happy but scary moment, you need time to think. To make any publishing or recording deal on any song is a Big Deal, and the faster you rush in, the longer you may regret your haste. So stall your caller, politely, of course; say you're due at an appointment but will call back in the afternoon, that you need to speak to your lawyer, that you'd like to come to their office, or that you'd like a confirmatory letter, e-mail, or fax. Say anything but get off the phone. Then review this chapter.

If you achieve any success as a songwriter, you will sign *contracts* on your songs, different contracts for different purposes. *Contract* can be a scary word that conjures up images of mustachioed villains forcing Mary Trueheart to sign away the deed to her ranch. When I first read a contract, my eyes glaze over as I try to penetrate the thicket of long words in fine print. Somewhere deep in the foreign royalty clauses, I am sure, lies a hidden paragraph that will mean I've signed away my life for a nickel.

Well, let's take a deep breath. Contracts are not as bad as all that. A contract means an agreement between two or more people on something. "Let's have lunch at Joe's Monday." "Sure. One o'clock?" "One o'clock, see you there"— that's a contract. A good contract helps both parties reach their own goals.

By this point you have undoubtedly made many performance contracts, most of them verbal: "August 6, nine to midnight, three forty-minute sets, $300." Then, when the boss says, "We still got a crowd, play to one" you can say, "Our deal was to midnight," and get an extra hundred bucks out of the guy.

There are three basic principles of making good contracts:

> Know what you are agreeing to.
> Know what you are not agreeing to.
> Know what you will get for what you give.

Pay attention to every contract. Make no commercial commitment about your work carelessly or on a whim. Some contracts are more crucial than others, however. Some present few pitfalls; others present many. The risks of making contracts increase with their dollar value—$50,000 deals live in another universe from $500 deals. Less obviously, the risks of making contracts increase with *time*. Performance contracts are easy to make because they are short contracts, for a night, a week, a two-month summer season at a hotel. If you make a bad deal, you can treat it as a learning experience that will soon be over. Song contracts are hard to make because *song contracts are long contracts.*

How long? Quite likely, if your song succeeds, for the rest of your life and a long time after that. Soon we'll go into detail, but note this crucial fact now: most publisher–songwriter contracts last for the length of the copyright if the song gets recorded; only songs that don't get recorded get returned to their writers. If "Shake It, Sexy Lady" is the platinum smash you think it is, the contract you are considering may be in force forever. Getting back what you sign away today could take many years and lawyers and dollars (and much luck).

If you love your songs as I love mine, selling them is an emotional matter. We want our songs to find good homes where they'll be valued and will thrive through decades, not get skimmed for a few quick bucks then stuck in a storage closet, with us on the outside powerless to rescue and revive them. On the other hand, to get our songs out to the world, we know we've got to let them go, give up the sole ownership that comes with authorship and share our songs with others who will, from then on, have as much or more to say and do about their future than we will. Anyone might well teeter nervously on such a brink, not sure which way to jump, not sure who and what to trust.

In the end, however, if you want to get your songs out to the world, you'll have to trust certain artists, producers, and publishers, and you'll have to sign contracts with them. Your goal is to make signing a song contract as little a leap in the dark as possible but, instead, a well-prepared move with risks and rewards you've carefully weighed, and which you've decided, on balance, is a good idea. Here are a few tips on how to reach that ideal spot:

- Learn all you can about the party you're dealing with. Knowledge is power. Visit their website, research their track record in the trade magazines. Discuss the deal with your friends and mentors in the business; they'll have valuable ideas and advice based on experience. Keep asking the other party questions until you know the whole score.
- Have a lawyer expert in copyright and intellectual property law review all song contracts you're offered, at least until you know the ropes. Pay willingly for the time it takes for him or her to put a contract's legalese into English you understand.
- Negotiate. Daily life doesn't give most of us much experience in negotiating. At stores we pay the listed price without question. Business, however, is all negotiation. Taking the first terms offered, "Sure, anything you say, Mr. Publisher," will mark you as an amateur and guarantee you the worst possible deal. Like poker, negotiation is a game of bluff and counter-bluff, and you won't learn overnight when to hold 'em and when to fold 'em. The best way to begin negotiation is to state your points in positive terms—"I want…I like.."—not in terms that carry criticisms—"I don't want… I don't like." The other party may respond, "We're offering you the standard contract, take it or leave it." If you come back, "I want to take it, but I do see a few things we might improve…" you may not get all you hope for, but you might get a piece, and the other party will know she is talking to a pro.
  Now two major warnings about negotiating:
  - *In negotiation, clout counts.* All contracts come down to who gets how much of every dollar earned under the contract. The more clout any party of the contract has, the more cents per dollar that party is going to get. Beginners with no track record have no clout. Accept the fact that the first contracts you sign will be less advantageous than contracts you may sign later.
  - *It's always a buyers' market in songwriting.* New songs flood daily into the marketplace, always exceeding what the marketplace can absorb. When publishers, producers, and A&R men smell hits, they can go to extravagant lengths to woo a writer, but week in, week out, they are drowned in demos, many of them excellent. Song-buyers stroll through the marketplace, picking and choosing

songs as they please, while we lowly song-sellers jump and dance and offer discounts to draw their attention. That's a second tough fact to accept, but take it to heart or you'll be constantly frustrated by unrealistic expectations. Instead, make the best deals you can while you keep working to improve your marketplace status and bargaining power.

- Go with the response you get. If you send demos out to ten buyers and get ignored by nine but called back by one, go with that one, even if it's your least favorite. Getting that call means that by some lucky chance, you have generated the crucial first spark of buyer interest. Your job now is to fan that spark into a flame. Negotiate, yes, but negotiate your way into a deal, not out of one. Keep the party polite. Anger and arguments will get you nowhere. Project a "we can work this out" attitude; walk away from the table only as a last resort. Making one deal can lead to another deal. No deal leaves you stuck at square one.

- Accept the consequences of the contracts you sign. So you make a mistake that comes back to haunt you? Well, everybody makes mistakes. Don't be too tough on yourself. Remember your mistakes well enough to learn from them; otherwise, let them go.

Now let's look at some of the song contracts you may sign.

Collaboration Contracts

A collaboration contract is a special contract because it's between you and a composer or lyricist who you know well enough to work with closely, perhaps an old friend and trusted colleague. You jam with Johnny one day, and almost by accident a song starts to takes shape, both of you kicking in ideas. Suddenly you've got a joint composition, "Words and music by Jenny Smith and Johnny Jones." A fun afternoon, but when you start selling the song, the fun can go flat. Who contributed how much? Maybe you got most of the song together, but Johnny came up with the killer hook. Do you think his input balances yours? Does he agree?

The basic rule on collaboration contracts is: *give credit where credit is due.* Make the percentages reflect as accurately as possible each collaborator's contribution; don't ask for a bigger piece, and don't accept a smaller piece, of a song than you deserve. John Lennon and Paul McCartney might never have fallen out so bitterly had they insisted that their song credits reflect who really wrote the songs—"Michelle" by Paul, "Norwegian Wood" by John—instead of lumping them all together as "Lennon and McCartney" songs.

Assigning credit among collaborators is easy if one collaborator writes the lyrics and another the music. That's a 50–50 split. If one writes the music and half the lyrics, that's a 75–25 split. But what do you do when one person has a good idea and the other works the idea into a song? Or if the second collaborator polishes a song already well-started by the first? Cases like this you'll have to negotiate with your partner. Here are a few rules of thumb.

If a non-songwriting pal says something catchy like, "It's gonna be a month of Mondays" and you, with no further help from him, turn that into a song, that's your song. If a songwriting pal says the same thing and keeps bugging you with ideas until the song is done, you'll share the song. If another musician shows you a cool chord sequence which you, over time, work into your hands and eventually use in a song, that's your song. If she shows you the same lick and you build a song together on the spot, that's a shared song. If you come up with the meat of a song and a pal supplies a few finishing touches, you could generously offer to share credit, or your pal could generously say, "No, it's your song, I was just reacting as a friend." Defend your interests when you negotiate song shares, but don't split hairs. A good song written by two people inseparably melds the inputs of its collaborators. Even if both writers privately think, "My ideas really make the song," a song that two writers create is best split 50–50.

If you do collaborate often with another writer and begin to write songs you'd like to demo and send out, sign a collaboration contract that defines the percentages each owns of each song and anything else that's important to both of you. This could be a simple letter of agreement that you and your partner sit down and write together, but show it to a lawyer and revise it as he or she suggests. If you are more active in the biz than your partner, ask to be in charge of selling the song with a percentage for your efforts and expenses. Certainly try to get the publishing for your company if you have one. If you both have companies, you can co-publish.

Publisher–Songwriter Contracts

Publisher–songwriter contracts are the most common and important song contracts of all, so read what follows with particular care.

As we discussed in *Business Basics*, songs reach the marketplace through publishers. If you do not start your own publishing company to represent your songs for sale, you will need to sign a *songwriter contract with a music publisher.*

The essence of most songwriter contracts is:

1. The songwriter sells ownership of a song to the publisher.
2. The publisher gets the right to market the song as it sees fit.
3. The publisher splits income received from the song 50–50 with the writer.

"Cut and dried," you say. ""What's to negotiate?" A lot. Let's start looking for wiggle room by going through a standard "Publisher Popular Song Contract" clause by clause.

Standard Publisher Popular Song Contract

This, with variations, is what a publisher will offer you to publish a single song. Certainly don't sign a contract that offers you less than this one does. As we go, I'll comment and point out places where you may be able to improve the terms.

> **Clause One declares that with this contract the Writer (you) "sells, assigns, transfers, and delivers" an unpublished original song by the writer, "including the title, words and music, and all copyrights" to the Publisher "for the full terms of all ... renewals and extensions of copyrights."**

That's why I said song contracts are long contracts. You will want to set certain limits to the length of the contract (see Clause Seven for the terms of *reversion*), but the fact remains that if the song makes money and the publisher pays you your share, you are selling your song and will not own it again. (It can be possible to buy a song back from a publisher; if the song's been successful, you'll pay a hefty price.)

> **In Clauses Two and Three, the writer affirms that the song is original and subject to no other contract.**

If you are honest, these present no problem.

> **Clause Four states what the Publisher agrees to pay the Writer for the song. Subsection A grants "$_____" as an "nonreturnable advance against royalties."**

This means a check when you sign the contract that you won't have to give back if the song stiffs, but which will be taken out of your royalties if it succeeds. You may face tough opposition, but try to get some money on signing. If they want the song so badly, they can put some cash on the table.

> Subsections B and C grant "_____ cents per copy" for sheet music sales of single songs and compilation songbooks.

Sheet music is seldom a big earner these days, but insist on ten percent of the retail price for printed music of your song. Of course, you'll share the ten percent compilation songbook income with the other writers.

> Subsection D grants the Writer "50 percent of any and all net sums actually received by the Publisher" from recording the song on records, movies, television, and other electronic means.

This is the famous writer-publisher 50–50 split. Accept no less. But note that little word "**net.**" That means that the publisher can pay you fifty percent *after* deducting some of the costs incurred in selling the song: making and duping demos, office expenses, travel, and so forth. Publishers argue that since they and the writers share the income 50–50, the two parties should share the expenses of making the income. The trouble is, some publishers take net to mean they can spend money as they please and make you foot the bill. Ask for fifty percent of the **gross,** truly all the money the publisher receives for your song. You probably won't get gross, but do hang in until you know what expenses can and cannot be legitimately deducted from your fifty percent share.

> Subsection E grants the Writer 50 percent of any other sales and use of the song—except that the Publisher does not need to share its Publisher income from ASCAP or BMI with the Writer.

Fine, but likewise, you don't need to share your ASCAP or BMI songwriter income with the publisher, and don't agree to under any circumstances. What you get from a performance rights society as a writer comes to you direct and is yours, all yours.

> Subsection F says the Publisher doesn't pay royalties on promotional copies.

This is no problem; any company needs to give some product away for publicity purposes.

Subsection G says the Publisher pays no royalties for "public performance" of a song.

Fine. The money you will earn from people playing your song at clubs and concerts will come from ASCAP or BMI.

Clause Five allows collaborators to state the share of the song each owns and to be paid accordingly.

This is no problem if you are satisfied with the share you've worked out with your writing partner or partners.

Clause Six commits the Publisher to sending the Writer twice-yearly royalty statements that detail how much has been earned with a check for any balance due.

That clause is often given time and dollar limits, such as "...after the first two years the publisher need not send a statement unless a balance is due or unless the balance reaches $100." This saves the publisher paperwork, but also gives the publisher a dangerous power. Let's say your song stops earning money after a few years, and you get used to no statements or checks coming in. Then the song becomes a minor hit in Denmark. The publisher gets a check but, figuring you'll never find out, conveniently forgets to send you your share. This has happened before and will happen again. Four ways to prevent it:

- Ask for royalty statements, no matter how much income earned, once a year.
- Ask for the right to get royalty statements on demand if you have received no statement for a year or more.
- Compare your royalty statements with your ASCAP or BMI statements. If ASCAP reports a surge of radio play in Denmark but you hear nothing from the publisher, then something's rotten and it ain't in Denmark.
- Keep careful records. Store your contracts in a safe but convenient file. Keep your royalty statements in neat chronological order. Note what you receive and when you receive it in a ledger. Make a calendar with crucial contractual dates clearly marked. Many publishers have counted on songwriters keeping such sloppy records that they could never prove how much they were owed. Do not be that foolish. Stay on top of the status of all your songs under contract.

Clause Seven allows ownership of the song to revert to the Writer if after one year the Publisher has not been able to get it recorded or otherwise used commercially.

This is the crucial *reversion clause*, and you must insist on it. Whether the ownership of a song reverts to you after one year or two, or whether you have to ask for reversion or get it automatically at a certain date—these details matter less than getting reversion in one form or another clearly spelled out. A good reversion clause is your only club to make the publisher get out there and sell your song. They lose any song they can't get recorded. Some songs stiff not because they're bad but because the publisher didn't know what to do with them. If you get your song back, you can try again with a new publisher who might make it click

In Clause Eight the Writer gives the Publisher permission to change, edit, transpose, rearrange "the setting of the words to the music and of music to the words," including changing the title, "as the Publisher deems desirable."

This is a sweeping, scary clause. A publisher could turn "I Love New York" into "You Hate LA," and you couldn't do anything about it. That seldom happens, however. In general, the clause gives the publisher the right to polish and improve a song, shape it to fit a certain artist or audience. Many songwriters say that savvy publishers often come up with the last-minute edits that make songs succeed. If their tweaking helps you get a hit, why complain? Still, fight for the right to approve major changes. As important, finish a song before you offer it. Publishers won't want to change a song that's already in the pocket.

Clause Nine declares that demands and notices other than royalty statements, from the Writer to the Publisher or vice versa, shall be sent by registered mail.

Fine. That simply gives both sides official proof of the dates important business letters were mailed.

Clause Ten makes the Publisher responsible for legal costs of any suit against someone who infringes on the song copyright, but allows the Publisher to deduct a share of the costs from the Writer's share of any money recovered by the suit.

Fair enough, but some publishers will try to pay a reduced royalty on money recovered from suits. Hold firm to the standard 50 percent for all income.

Clauses Eleven and Twelve make the Publisher the commercial center of the song, able to negotiate and sign all further contracts and agreements for the song.

This spells out certain rights of ownership already outlined in Clause One.

Clause Thirteen gives the Publisher the right "to assign this agreement and its obligations ... to any person, firm, or corporation."

This clause gives the Publisher a masked power that exposes how little power the songwriter has. Let's say you sell Bill at New York's Alpha Music a song because, over many sales calls, you and Bill have become buddies. You speak to Bill every few weeks to check on the song's progress. Then Bill gets fired. The new guy at Bill's desk doesn't dig your material, and he sells your song with a grab-bag of others to Omega Music in LA where nobody knows you. The song gets lost in the shuffle. Now trying to keep tabs on it means long distance calls to answering machines that don't call back.

Song contracts, Clause Thirteen reveals, are commodities. As you sold your song to a publisher, that publisher can sell the song to another publisher, and they do so all the time, sometimes selling a few songs, sometimes the company's whole catalog. Publishers like Warner Brothers grow huge by buying up smaller publishers and their songs. The new publisher still must abide by the original contract, but assigning and reassigning can dislocate a song from its roots, leaving it like a baseball player traded from one team to another, always a stranger in a new hometown.

Try to get the right to bar the publisher from selling your song as a single entity without your approval, but you are unlikely to succeed, particularly early in your career. In general, publishers want to own songs the way you own furniture or a car: yours, once you've paid for them, to keep or dispose of as you see fit.

Clauses Fourteen and Fifteen declare the state, usually New York, Tennessee, or California, under whose laws the contract will be interpreted, and declare that the contract will be binding on both parties, their heirs, or successor companies.

If the contract is a good one, these present no problem.

Songwriters Guild of America Popular Songwriters Contract

Publishers wrote the contract we've just reviewed to benefit themselves. Fortunately, the Songwriters Guild of America, a voluntary association of songwriters founded in 1931, has written a contract to benefit us, dealing with the same issues as the publishers' contract, but at every point defending our interests and expanding our percentages. You can get a free copy of the SGA contract by writing to the Guild. The New York, Nashville, and Los Angeles offices are listed in the Appendix and you may use the SGA contract, in whole or in part, even if you are not a member. When you write, ask for information about the Guild. Joining now or later could be a wise move.

Let's review the significant ways in which the SGA contract differs from the standard contract.

Signing the SGA contract also "assigns, transfers, and delivers" the copyright of a song to a publisher but for a limited time:

> "... (no more than 40) years from the date of the contract or 35 years from ... the first release of a commercial sound recording."

That's automatic reversion, even if the song has become a richly earning evergreen. Much better, obviously, than the publisher's contract but hard to get. Understand that since song copyrights cost nothing to store and do not get eaten by moths or mice, publishers don't mind owning them through long non-earning years. Someday, they figure, a director will make film about long-ago 2004 and use "Shake It Sexy Lady" to capture the sound of the era. Then the long dormant tune will wake and make money again. If you sign the SGA contract and that film director comes along forty-one years later, you or your heirs, not the publisher, will own the rights and reap the whole reward.

The next big difference comes in the royalty advance clause:

> "[The] advance on royalties ... shall be deductible only from payments ... due the Writer under this contract."

The crucial words here are "**under this contract.**" Let's say you get a good relationship going with BimBam Music and sell them a dozen songs over a few years, getting about $500 each in advances and demo expenses. None of them do much, so you owe the publisher $5000 or so—not that you have to pay it back, but still a debt. Song thirteen gets lucky, makes a little noise, and you rip open your first royalty statement thinking, "Now we're going to Paris like we've always dreamed," but find a dismal check for $11.52. Number thirteen has barely paid back the other twelve advances.

Cross-collateralization is the big word for making earnings under one contract repay advances due on other contracts. The SGA's "under this contract" blocks the practice. Try to get cross-collaterization out of your contracts; push hard enough and you may succeed.

The SGA contract sets 10 percent as a minimum royalty for sheet music sales, but adds "escalators" that increase the royalty up to 15 percent as sales rise. More importantly, the contract asks for, **in no case, less than "50 percent of all gross receipts of the Publisher" for the song**.

There's that **net–gross** difference we noted earlier. One advantage of gross is simplicity. The publisher takes in $1000, and you get $500. You can see this on the statement, no muss no fuss. A royalty statement peppered with expenses you didn't authorize and can't verify can leave you with a much reduced check and many questions you'll never get answered. Fight for gross, but you may not get it.

The SGA contracts make reversion automatic:

> **If a song has not been recorded and commercially released in a period "not exceeding twelve months … this contract shall terminate, and "all copyrights … shall automatically … become the property of the Writer."**

This means you don't have to send any registered letters to get your song back. If the publisher hasn't placed your song in a year, it's yours again to sell elsewhere. With the exception that if the publisher pays you a second advance or *bumper* of $250 or more, then the publisher gets to keep the song for another six months.

The SGA contract also demands that royalty statements be sent within forty-five days after the accounting period ends—some publishers can be snail-slow in sending statements—and that those statements must detail where the song income has come from: records by which artists, movies, television, foreign, and so forth. You also can demand to examine the publisher's books to make sure that their accounting is accurate. These and similar demands scattered through the contract block loopholes in the standard contract, but they also tie the publisher's hands. You may well not be able to win on such points.

The two most important of these demands are, first:

> **Writer's Consent to Licenses—the Publisher must get written consent of the Writer to license the song for "exclusive use" or to be used in a movie or television show.**

You've surely heard stories about songwriters who've been shocked to hear their pro-ecology song used in a car commercial or their most romantic ballad underscoring a raunchy scene in a porno film. When they complain to the publisher, they find there's nothing they can do. "Writer's Consent to Licenses" gives you something you can do; you can say no before it happens.

And second:

> **The Publisher may not sell or assign the song "without the written consent of the Writer" unless the Publisher is selling its entire catalog.**

This means that the publisher can sell your song if it's going out of business or merging with another company, but cannot use your song as a trading card, selling it to make a little cash in a slow season. You are signing a contract on your song, the SGA contract explains, relying "on the personal service and ability of the Publisher" you are signing with. It is "the essence of the relationship" that the rights granted "shall remain with the Publisher…and not pass to any other person." This valuable provision will keep your song from floating here and there in the music marketplace. It's a tough provision to get, though, because, I'll say again, publishers like to own songs outright and don't want to consult the writer on each and every deal they make.

The standard contract and the SGA contract define the lower and upper limits of songwriter–publisher negotiation. You'll never do better than the SGA, and don't accept worse than the standard. Quite likely, you'll start with the standard contract and step-by-step improve it in the SGA direction.

Exclusive Songwriter Term Contract

An exclusive songwriter contract is like a single song contract except that it's for all the songs the writer creates for the length of the contract, usually one year with options to renew:

> **"The Publisher agrees to pay the Writer … \$_____ dollars per week as a nonreturnable advance to be deducted from any and all royalties" for all songs, words and music, that the Writer "shall have invented, written, conceived … created or originated heretofore or during the full term" of the contract.**

The crucial word here is "heretofore." With it the publisher is saying, "We'll own the songs you will write *and* own all the songs you've ever written that don't already have a publisher." One signature and they own every song you ever wrote? That sounds scary; so let's take a calmer look at the matter.

Signing an exclusive songwriter contract could be a wonderful, life-changing event for you, a huge step toward becoming a successful pop songwriter.

Contract writers are craftsmen of whom good work is expected, cats who know music and the marketplace. If an on-the-square publisher with a track record in your style offers you an exclusive writing contract, that's a gold ring. Grab it.

To mine that gold, you'll need to show the publisher the best songs you've got, new or old. Hopefully, the steady paycheck will inspire a flood of fresh masterpieces. You'll also dig into your bag of finished, unfinished, and barely started songs. Now they'll have a chance to reach the audience they deserve. On your first day under contract, you'll think, "This company just had a rockabilly hit. Now's the time to dust off 'Honky Tonk Saturday Night' and finally give it a decent bridge." Publishers know every songwriter has a bag of songs like yours, and since there's no way to prove when a song is conceived, they claim ownership of all the writer's songs, "whenever invented, written, or originated." Yet publishers won't go rooting in your desk drawers to find songs you wrote ten years ago. They'll hear only those songs you offer them under the contract, and they'll end up owning only those songs that earn some money—in exclusive contracts as well as in a single-song contract, *insist on reversion for songs that don't get recorded.*

If you already want to hoard your best work ("I'm not so sure of these guys, I'll keep 'Honky Tonk Saturday Night' under my hat"), maybe signing an exclusive writing contract isn't the gold ring for you. Self-publishing or selling songs one-by-one may suit you better. If your doubts persist, think twice or three times before becoming an exclusive writer. On the other hand, when your exclusive contract runs out, you may offer any songs you've still got in your bag to a new publisher.

Final caution: watch out for the *options clause*. A one-year contract usually includes a clause giving the publisher the choice to sign you for another year. So if after a year the publisher is unhappy with you, they can drop you, but if you're unhappy with them, you still may be stuck for a second year. Try to get the options clause dropped from your contract. If that's not possible, try to set a minimum level before it can be used. They'll have the option to renew only if you earn X dollars or get X number of songs recorded.

Licensing Contracts

Songwriter–publisher contracts are *selling contracts*, agreements in which the songwriter sells ownership of a song to the publisher. Then the publisher tries to make *licensing contracts*, agreements that, for specified fees, grant licenses to people and companies who want to use the song in specified ways: record it, include it in movie soundtrack, feature its hook in an advertising jingle, sample its bass line, or print it in a songbook. Licensing contracts are in essence *rental contracts*, agreements in which the publisher owns a song and rents out its uses just as a landlord owns a building and rents out its apartments. When the tenants move out, the landlord still owns the building. When the TV series goes off the air, the publisher still owns the theme song.

Many kinds of song uses can be licensed, and with the digital revolution, the number will only increase. Each licensed use is a potential earning stream for your songs, but remember that publishers, not songwriters, sign licensing contracts. If you self-publish, you'll negotiate your song licenses yourself. If you sell your songs to a publisher, the publisher will deal with the record or film company and pay you fifty percent of the licensing income. To get a grasp on what you may do yourself or what your publisher will do for you, let's review a song's most important licensing contracts.

Mechanical License

A mechanical license is a license to record a song, to make a mechanically reproduced image of music in a permanent medium. "Mechanical license" recalls the days when records were shellac discs played on phonographs with big horns and sturdy steel needles following wiggly grooves, and the term is still used today though records have evolved into ghostly bits and bytes floating in the twilight of computer hard drives.

Getting records made of our songs, "cuts" they call them in Nashville, is, of course, what we're all chasing. Even better than cuts are "covers," multiple recordings of the same song. Errol Garner's "Misty" has been covered thousands of times, each one a mechanical license. I wish you many cuts and covers!

US copyright law gives the publisher the right to pick who gets a song's first mechanical license. Until a song has been commercially recorded, it can be recorded only by permission of its owner. After a song has been recorded once, however, anyone can record it without asking permission if they pay a *compulsory license fee* which, as 2004 begins, is 8.5 cents per copy of the song.

Over years, the compulsory license figure has become the seldom-paid maximum fee to record a song. Most people who record songs don't pay the compulsory fee. Instead, they ask permission and negotiate a license with its publisher, paying a figure just below or way below 8.5 cents a copy, depending on clout.

Mechanical license contracts are relatively simple. They state the agreed royalty per copy and the payment period, quarterly in general practice. Still, sign no mechanical license without showing the contract to your lawyer. Note that record companies will ask for a hidden discount, the payment of royalties on 90 percent of copies sold. That much you'll probably have to give them, but say no to more. Keep an eye, too, on the percentage of promotional copies allowed. Record companies have been known to avoid paying royalties by selling "promo copies" under the table.

If your publisher, whether that's you or a company you've sold a song to, does get more than a few cuts and covers, keeping track of how much is owed by whom and when is it due can become a daunting task, especially if some of the records were made abroad and foreign rights and subrights come into play. A one-man publisher has no chance of policing today's international record market. Fortunately, The Harry Fox Agency (its address is in the Appendix) and several similar companies exist just for that purpose. They keep tabs on and collect every dollar that domestic and foreign record companies owe publishers. Thousands of small and mid-sized publishers gladly pay The Harry Fox Agency a six percent fee on all mechanical license income the agency collects; they know that without Harry Fox much of that income would never come in.

Synchronization License

A synchronization license is a license to use a song in a film, synchronized with a moving picture image. Songs, as you surely know, play a major role in films of all kinds. TV sitcoms and police dramas have theme songs, and movies play songs under the opening and closing credits. Many film songs have become hits, the great example of this being "As Time Goes By" from the Humphrey Bogart–Ingrid Bergman masterpiece, *Casablanca*. Since director Martin Scorcese's groundbreaking *Mean Streets* in the 1970s, entire film scores have been fashioned from pop songs, and directors routinely use songs coming from a radio or a jukebox to set a movie's era. A few bars of "Boogie-Woogie Bugle Boy" says World War II, and "When You're Going to San Francisco" takes us back to 1967, the Summer of Love.

Synchronization licenses (and the accompanying *performance license* that gives the filmmaker the right to show the movie to the public) are generally paid as flat fees. Once paid, the filmmaker may keep the song married to the film as long as the film copyright lasts. Film songs, like actors, are valued by how they appear in the film. They are valued little if they appear as nearly invisible threads in the background soundtrack, more if their source is shown, a cocktail pianist playing the song at a party, for example, still more if the song is featured and repeated at key moments, and most of all if it's a title song like "Love Is a Many-Splendored Thing."

If a song plays a major role in a movie, the filmmaker may well ask for an *exclusive license* that bars the publisher from selling the same song to be featured in a competing movie. That's no problem if you agree that the song will be deeply identified with the first film, and the filmmaker pays well for the privilege. As a rule, however, the wise publisher will grant *non-exclusive licenses*, which allow the filmmaker to use the song in his film but allow the publisher to make any other synchronization deal that comes into the office.

What song synchronization licenses can earn varies widely due to the interplay of many factors. The film's overall budget, the size of the studio, and the fame of the song are three of the most important. Use in a film is a wonderful opportunity for any song, but before signing any synchronization license, do your research into the filmmaker and his production company, and show the contract to your lawyer. Good news: The Harry Fox Agency also collects synchronization royalties.

Theatrical or Grand Rights License

Songs in a live show like a Broadway musical require a *theatrical* or *grand rights license*, which grants the show's producers the right to use the songs when the show is performed in a theater. Grand rights licenses are nearly always royalty deals, a percentage of the show's income, but the size of the percentages varies greatly, and the attendant clauses of exclusivity, film rights, soundtrack options and the like get complex. The Dramatists Guild (songwriters are welcome; the address is in the Appendix) is your best resource for information on grand rights contracts. A basic tip, though, is that it's okay to accept a flat fee from a nonprofit theater planning ten performances, but for open-ended runs in commercial theaters, make sure you get a royalty deal based on ticket price, theater size, and the length of run. Also, get an advance.

Print License

Few music publishers actually print music books. Instead they grant other companies the right to make and sell books that include the publisher's songs. Hal Leonard of Milwaukee is perhaps the largest American firm that licenses the songs of many publishers, then groups the songs in collections that appeal to the music-book-buying public. Seldom a major income stream, print licenses can be slow and steady earners that have paid many a small publisher's light bill month after month. The publisher's standard percentage is ten percent of a music book's suggested retail price, divided pro rata with the other publishers whose songs are in the book. When the wonderful day comes that a music book publisher wants to put out a songbook of your greatest hits, you might push that percentage up a notch or two.

Jingle Licenses

Jingle licenses grant advertisers the right to use songs in radio and television commercials. Many songwriters and music publishers specialize in writing and selling jingles, and many others gladly discover that advertisers want to use decade-old hits to boost the popularity of their products. Jingle income can be enormous, and to simplify a highly complex subject, licensed songs earn more or less depending on the prominence of a song's use, the length of the spot, whether the singers are seen on screen, what markets the spot will play in, and how many times a week and for how many months the spot runs. At the risk of repeating myself, if a jingle opportunity arises, do your research and show the contract to your lawyer.

Internet and Digital Use Licenses

Music and digital technology married in the '80s, giving birth to the CD, DAT tape, and sampling. Music and the Web married in the '90s, giving birth to file-sharing, Napster, and a million songwriter web sites. As 2004 rolls on, the marriages and births continue apace, often accompanied by money squabbles and lawsuits. The digital revolution is changing the music business so rapidly that today's facts often become tomorrow's irrelevancies. Music creators love the miraculous powers of digital recording, and music sellers love the Internet's worldwide market, but both are still trying to figure out how to license the many digital uses of music. Who owns a bass line? Who owns a synth sound? How can you license and get paid for songs released to the World Wide Web? Two tips:

- Keep your eye on the headlines. To earn money from Internet and digital use licenses, you and your publisher need to stay abreast of the latest court decisions, the newest marketing tools and opportunities. A sampling license for a fragment of one of your songs may someday earn you more than the original song. Many songwriter–publishers are selling their songs by enticing fans to visit their web sites and pay, voluntarily, for song downloads. Websites like CDBaby.com are becoming virtual record stores. New companies are gathering thousands of Web-use song licenses for on-line distribution.
- Make the Web and digital licenses you sign as specific as possible. The digital revolution is so unpredictable and open-ended that vagueness in a digital license now could cost you and your publisher money later. Get language into all your licensing contracts specifically reserving web and digital use rights to yourself. You don't want a film company that only licensed synchronization rights using your song on its website for free.

Be specific. That makes a good ending to our discussion of song licensing. Licensing contracts, we said, are like rental contracts, the publisher like a landlord. If a landlord wants no pets in his rental apartments, he must write a lease that says so. If he doesn't want the tenant to move in her whole family, he's got to put in an occupancy limit clause. A publisher must be just as specific: US and Canada but not world rights, movie but not video rights, network but not cable rights. Until the first license is signed, remember, a publisher owns all the rights to a song. After making a licensing deal, the publisher still owns every right not granted under the license. Make sure that your licensing contracts spell out that crucial point: "The Publisher reserves all rights except those specified in this contract."

Co-Publishing and Administration Contracts

So far, for purposes of clarity, we've spoken of publishing yourself and selling to an established publisher as separate, alternative paths. Now is the time to admit that in practice the boundaries between the two are often blurred.

Who publishes a song comes down to percentages. Songwriters, publishers, producers, artists, and record companies, everybody in the business knows that getting and holding onto a song's publishing, half of its earnings, can be worth huge amounts of money. Everybody, therefore, wants a piece of the publishing. If Steve Superstar hears "Shake It, Sexy Lady" and says, "I love it, let's record it," you can be sure that you'll soon be talking to Steve's manager Tony Toughguy, who will say, "Of course, Superstar Music, Steve's company, will get the publishing."

"Oh, no," you'll reply as firmly as you can, "I've got my own publishing company," only to be cut off by Tony's sarcastic sneer, "Yeah, right! Your songs have never sold more than ten thousand records, Steve's last five albums went platinum, but you'll keep the publishing? Tell me another."

As you reel from that body blow, remember: Tony may be bluffing. Superstar Music is probably not a music publishing company in the full sense of the word, a company with offices and a staff pitching demos. It may instead be a paperwork company created by Tony's lawyers as a percentage-raising concession that Steve has won with his platinum albums. A "real" publisher, WB or Sony-ATV, may own the biggest piece of Superstar Music and/or administer its day-to-day running for a fee.

That's why the answer to a simple question like "Who's got the publishing?" can get complicated fast. Everybody is fighting for a slice of the publishing pie, and they get a big slice, a little slice, a few crumbs of the crust, or nothing depending on clout.

If you, acting as your own publisher, sell a song license to an artist or company on your music biz success level, you may be able to keep all the publishing. That's one excellent reason to pitch first to local targets, not national stars. By the time you're talking with the big boys, your regional cuts and covers will give your publishing company more clout. When selling to an artist or company on a higher level than you're on, try for a *co-publishing contract* so your company will keep a piece, big or small, of the publishing earnings. If you get co-publishing, however, mostly likely the larger company will become the *administering publisher*, the office that handles the paperwork and gets sent the checks. Co-publishing with an administrating publisher is like being published by an established company, except that your royalty will be larger.

Negotiating your way between keeping all or none of the publishing will take nerves of steel and a very good lawyer. Good luck. Remember, as I said earlier, your early contracts will not be as advantageous as your later ones. Give yourself time to learn the ropes. Allow yourself a few mistakes.

Recording Artist Contracts

Recording artist contracts are not, strictly speaking, song contracts but they deserve mention because most singer–songwriters, myself included, would love to become recording stars, known and loved for singing our original songs. A record company A&R man spots you as an up-and-comer. Working with your manager, the label helps shape, focus, and bring out your innate talent, at the same time launching you with a coordinated series of CDs, concert tours, and flattering publicity campaigns. Under this kind of treatment, you, like the Beatles, Bob Dylan, Stevie Wonder, Aretha Franklin, and Billy Joel before you, might grow in creative directions you could never achieve without a record company's consistent, long-term support.

Every day was not peaches-and-cream for The Beatles and Bob Dylan at their labels, and some of the horror stories you've heard are true. Artists have woken up after the hits stopped coming to find that they owed their label pots of money. Less known but more common are the quiet success stories of labels who stick by midlevel singer–songwriters though decades, giving them, through their ups and down, a home, an outlet, and a connection to their fans. It's the rare (and foolish) singer–songwriter who walks away from a recording contract. The problem, if anything, is hiding our eagerness at the bargaining table: "Sure I'll sign, just make me a star."

Recording artist contracts have dozens of provisions for royalties, guarantees, options, recording advances, dates of delivery, promotional support, and on and on. Record deals vary widely with the size of the label, the size of the market (jazz artists sign smaller contracts than rock artists) and many other factors, including the age of the artist (younger artists get the multi-album development deals, older artists accept album-by-album deals). I'll say again, more forcibly than ever: CONSULT A LAWYER EXPERT IN THE FIELD BEFORE SIGNING ANY RECORDING ARTIST CONTRACT.

The gold you glimpse in signing a record deal may hypnotize you, but snap out of it enough to *remember your songs*. If you and your prospective label consider your writing central to your appeal, your songs will be central to your recording contract and can tremendously increase your earnings. Non-writing singers may get a 10 percent artist's royalty for a record. Singer–songwriters get the same 10 percent plus the songwriter's royalty, ASCAP or BMI earnings, and whatever publishing income they've been able to retain—bonuses that can more than double the non-writer's income and last far longer. You and your lawyer must ask how many original songs the label wants per album. Does the label want you to work with a collaborator to rewrite your songs? Do they get the right to reject original songs they don't like or think won't be commercial? Are they demanding that you assign your songs to their affiliated publisher? Who will own your songs when the recording deal runs out?

Keep asking these and other questions until you have answers that you understand, accept, and can see in the contract's black and white. You owe it to yourself, to your years of writing and rewriting, to value the contribution your songs make to your recording success. Protect your songs and get a fair price for the rights you part with. Remembering your songs when you sign a record deal will make you money, forgetting them will cost you money.

In this chapter, we've looked at many kinds of song contracts. By now you may be feeling stunned and confused by the facts and figures whirling in your head. Fortunately, you'll never have to sign all these contracts in one day. Learning the intricacies of the music biz is like mastering the intricacies of music. We go step-by-step from apprentice to journeyman and, if we're lucky, to master. You'll never know all the ins-and-outs, and you won't win every battle, but in time your competence and your confidence will grow.

Above all, keep learning and keep negotiating. "In the music biz," say wise old pros, "there's no such thing as a standard contract." Norms and accepted practices exist, but the old pros are right. In business, everything is up for grabs. Like a house, a table, or a book, a song is worth today only what you can get for it today. Accept the challenge of trying to make good deals on your songs. Do your best to increase your slice of the pie, but don't get greedy. Business people who let the other guy make a few bucks too, increase their own profits, make friends, and sleep soundly. Feel proud of every penny your music earns, but remind yourself daily that, wonderful as money is, you're in this business because you love to write songs, and you want the whole world to hear them. Writing songs is a tough way to make a million dollars, but we'll only succeed if, first, last, and always, we keep writing great songs.

chapter 16

Staying in Business

Little shops often spring up on our block in New York's East Village. Weeks before the opening, we see a cheerful guy or gal or couple bustling here and there, dressing the window and filling empty shelves, their bright eyes and smiles beaming confidence that their style in clothes or books or furniture or pastry is so delightful and original that the world will flock to their doors. The shop will always be full of people oohing and ahhing and buying and buying. Running a boutique will be such fun!

It is fun at the opening gala as friends crowd around and champagne corks fly. Then seasons pass, business slows to a trickle, and we see the anxious shop owner keeping ostentatiously busy as long hours go by and, out of all the passersby, no one enters even to take a look around. One shop catches on and lasts for years; another soon dwindles down to its final "50% OFF!!" signs and disappears. What's the difference between the two shops? The first shop managed to *stay in business.*

Any business person will tell you that starting a business is easy, staying in business is hard. Good times drown you, bad times starve you. Year in, year out, you've got to stay on top of your business, respond to changes in the market, keep one eye on the pennies and the other on the competition. You need sense and guts to know when to risk a good investment and when to walk way from a bad one. You have to have the pep to pull you through tough times and the brains not to go bananas when business is booming.

If you do keep trying, keep writing, keep performing, keep sending out demos no matter what, I guarantee you, you will stay in business. Somehow, sometime, one demo, one song, one performance, one promo package will stir somebody's interest. You'll follow up, get the gig, and click with someone you meet there. They'll sing one of your songs or show it to another artist who'll record it. That'll earn you a little write-up in a local paper, which you will photocopy and send to all your contacts. One of them, impressed by your growing fame, will call to offer another gig. The "Big Break" of legend may never come, but from a daisy chain of little breaks you'll build a steadily growing career.

Hard work, *planning*, and *setting realistic goals* are crucial to long-term business success. So is luck, though I've found that judicious application of the first three qualities can minimize bad luck and enhance good luck. Here are four tips for songwriting longevity from my experience:

- The buck stops with YOU. Being a singer–songwriter is an individual enterprise. I wish you helpful friends and colleagues, but you'll always be the axle of your own wheel. The gigs you don't book someone else will get. The demo or the press kit you don't send out won't land on a pile to be opened. Even if the wonderful day comes when PR people write your press releases and tour managers book your hotel rooms, you'll still want to be in charge of your image, set your own budgets, directions, and goals. Accept the challenge of managing your own career. When analyzing a problem, give blame where blame is due, but watch out for thinking it's always the other guy's fault—it isn't. If a competitor does do you wrong, it's up to you to protect your own interest.
- Tell the truth. Don't lie, boast, cheat, or steal, ever, under any circumstances. Keep your sales pitch and publicity materials confident and positive, but don't promise more than you can deliver. Honesty *is* the best policy. Telling the truth about your own mistakes can lead to moments of excruciating embarrassment, but you'll live through them and be calm again, knowing you told the truth. Lies confess weakness. The truth connects us to the unshakable strength of reality. A reputation for honesty is an enormous business asset. Don't do anything that will risk the trust you've built up with your colleagues. The great songwriter Bo Diddley put the whole matter in a few words, "Don't write a check with your mouth you can't cash with your ass."
- Defend your songwriting. In your early days especially, friends, family and colleagues may tease you about your efforts and your ambitions, laugh at your awkward rhymes, tell you that you are nuts to hope for success. An old college roommate comes to see you at the Hot Club and over coffee afterwards says, with a big smile, "Well, don't quit your day job."

  She's kidding right? Sure she is, but the line still stings. If you respond to every snide remark you hear as you push yourself forward as a songwriter, you'll soon exhaust yourself. Instead, let as much bullshit as possible go over your head. Let your own inner appraisal of your work sustain you as you keep studying to improve. Yet if the sniping from people close to you continues, take what steps are necessary to stop it. Don't let subtle, wounding criticism sap your confidence. Whether it be a mother or a brother or a spouse, speak up plainly. Say, "I love and am proud of my songwriting. If you're my friend, you'll be proud of it, too, or at least keep your mouth shut. If you keep putting down my music, we won't be friends anymore."

Music is an innocent activity that hurts no one. If you enjoy what you're doing, keep doing it proudly no matter what anybody says. If your pals think you're goofy, too bad for them. They won't get invited to Carnegie Hall on your big night.

On the other hand, don't quit your day job. Depending on your songwriting to earn your entire living could put too much pressure on your creativity and too much reliance on an unpredictable profession. Look for work that relates to music. Being a copyist, arranger, sideman, or music teacher will keep you in touch with your art. Being a secretary at a music publisher could do more for you than being a secretary at an architectural firm. Keep your expenses low. Be prudent, even cautious, in your investments. Debt has killed many a good business.

- You may not stick with songwriting, and if so, don't knock yourself. Hopes, dreams, and realities change with passing years. Goals important to you now—ASCAP checks, record sales, a foot in the door at Mega Music—may morph into new goals, family and kids, surfboarding, owning a restaurant, whatever. Perhaps, despite your yearnings, you're not really a songwriter at heart. Maybe you're writing songs because your parents either did or didn't want you to write songs, or because that's what the cool kids did at college. As you grow past early conflicts and discover your true self, emotions like that can fade away. If this happens to you, accept it, and go on eagerly to your new pursuits. But *never throw your songs away.* Another turn or two in your life and you may be singing them again.

Sometimes, I feel like a songwriting Johnny Appleseed. With a bag full of songs over my shoulder, I go here and there, planting a song or two anytime I see a bit of fertile ground. Will my little musical seedlings come up? I don't know, but the only chance they have is if I get them planted by hook or by crook. So I keep going, writing new songs, rewriting them, singing them, sending out demos and press kits, following up, and going with the response I get. Call me a nutty optimist, I don't care. I'm enjoying myself.

Remember the three cornerstones—love your craft, love yourself, and love other people—and you too will enjoy songwriting year after year. You'll be learning all the time, and the pride you feel in your expanding abilities will push you into new challenges. You'll be doing work you love, one of the great recipes for human happiness. You'll meet and work with interesting people from many walks of life, some of whom will become dear friends and close colleagues.

Who knows? Someday you may have a hit, two hits, or ten. The world will sing your songs and the money will come flowing in. I hope so for you as I hope so for myself. But if that grand come-and-get-it day never comes, well, we had a good time trying.

Appendix

Songwriters need information of all kinds—names, phone numbers, mail and e-mail addresses—and need all kinds of questions answered: Where does one get good legal advice? What's a fair rate at a studio? What's the effect of a new copyright law? What's the difference between the melodic and harmonic minor? The only way to learn what you need to know will be to ask questions and keep asking them until you get answers you need. "Asking is the key to success," a wise old pro once said. "Learn to live with rejection, and you can ask for anything."

This Appendix points you in directions where you will find answers. Below are addresses of songwriting groups and guilds you may want to join, books and magazines filled with basic facts and recent news, and other information sources for all kinds of legal and professional matters.

Copyright Registration

Web site: www.copyright.gov

Copyright Office
Library of Congress
Washington, D.C. 20559
202 707-3000

Songwriting and Publishing Groups and Guilds

American Society of Composers, Authors and Publishers (ASCAP)
Web site: ascap.com

Los Angeles:
7920 West Sunset Boulevard
Los Angeles, CA 90046
323-883-1000

Nashville:
Two Music Square West
Nashville, TN 37203
615-742-5000

New York:
One Lincoln Plaza
New York, NY 10023
212-621-6000

Broadcast Music Inc (BMI)
Web site: bmi.com

Los Angeles:
8730 Sunset Boulevard
3rd Floor West
West Hollywood, CA 90069
310-659-9109

Nashville:
10 Music Square East
Nashville TN 37203
615-401-2000

New York:
320 West 57th Street
New York, NY 10019
212-586-2000

Society of European State Authors and Composers (SESAC)

Web site: sesac.com

New York:
  421 West 54th Street
  New York, NY 10019
  212-586-3450

Nashville:
  55 Music Square East
  Nashville, TN 37203
  615-320-0055

Songwriters Guild of America (SGA)

Web site: songwriters.com

New York:
  1560 Broadway, Suite 1306
  New York, NY 10036
  212-786-7902
  201-867-7603

Nashville:
  615-329-1782

Los Angeles:
  213-462-1108

American Federation of Musicians (AF of M)

Los Angeles:
  7080 Hollywood Boulevard
  Los Angeles CA 90028
  213-251-4510

Nashville:
  11 Music Circle North
  Nashville, TN 37212
  615-244-9514

New York:
1501 Broadway Suite 600
New York, NY 10036
212-869-1330

The Dramatists Guild

1501 Broadway, Suite 701
New York NY 10036
212-398-9366

The Harry Fox Agency

711 3rd Avenue
New York, NY 10017
212-370-5330

Low-cost Legal Aid and Advice

Volunteer Lawyers for the Arts

Web site: vlany.org

1 East 53rd Street
New York, NY 10022
212-319-2787

There are legal aid organizations for artists in many states with lawyers on call for free or inexpensive consultation sessions. Look in the phone book for the one nearest you, or call or write the New York office for further directions.

How-to Books on Songwriting

Davis, Sheila. *The Craft of Lyric Writing*. Cincinnati: Writer's Digest Books, 1985.
   Excellent, detailed guide to lyric writing, based on years of successful teaching in New York, with many fascinating examples that show students' lyrics slowly progressing from rough drafts to finished work.

Hirschhorn, Joel. *The Complete Idiot's Guide to Songwriting*. Indianapolis: Pearson Education, 2001.
   A bit scattered, but still full of good suggestions from an experienced pro.

Leikin, Molly-Ann. *How to Write a Hit Song*. Milwaukee: Hal Leonard, 2000.
———. *How to Make a Good Song a Hit Song*. New York: Billboard Books, 1990.
A pair of good books on the basics by a contemporary working pro.

Liggett, Mark and Cathy. *The Complete Handbook of Songwriting: An Insider's Guide to Making It in the Music Industry*. New York: Plume, 1993.
A solid, informative book, stronger on the business than the creative end of the craft.

Peterik, Jim; Austin, Dave; Bickford, Mary Ellen. *Songwriting for Dummies*. New York: Wiley Publishing, 2002.
A nuts-and-bolts handbook with all the strengths (and weaknesses) of the "for dummies" genre.

Webb, Jimmy. *Tunesmith: Inside the Art of Songwriting*. New York: Hyperion, 1998.
A sometimes quirky, sometimes detailed look at songwriting and the songwriting life by a contemporary master.

Books on Music Theory

Brimhall, John. *Theory Notebook*. Miami: Hansen House, 1969.
A baby book compared to the Bibles listed below, this workbook's many exercises and examples will take you past all the early hurdles in writing and reading music.

Piston, Walter. *Harmony*. New York: W. W. Norton, 1969.
The third edition of *Harmony* was my Bible for music theory. Since then, it's been published in many revised editions. Piston wrote for students of classical music, but his fine book teaches the fundamentals of all Western music.

Mehegan, John. *Jazz Improvisation*. New York: Watson-Guptill Publications, 1965.
"Mehegan," as jazz cats call the four volumes of *Jazz Improvisation*, is the jazz harmony Bible. The first volume, *Tonal and Rhythmic Principles*, is the most valuable volume for songwriters. Get through that, and you'll know all you need to know to write great standards.

Appreciations of the Craft

Gottlieb, Robert, and Kimball, Robert. *Reading Lyrics*. New York: Pantheon Books, 2000.
A selective but still exhaustive compilation of lyrics from 1900–1950, with an emphasis on the great writers of Manhattan school: Irving Berlin, Ira Gershwin, Cole Porter, Dorothy Fields, and Alan Jay Lerner. It will repay countless readings whether close or causal.

Wilder, Alec. *American Popular Song: The Great Innovators 1900–1950*. New York: Oxford University Press, 1972.
A classic study of American popular music, filled with illuminating musical examples.

Zinsser, William. *Easy to Remember: The Great American Songwriters and Their Stories*. Boston: David R. Godine. 2000.
An affectionate appreciation of Tin Pan Alley traditions by a noted writer who's also a fine amateur pianist.

Zollo, Paul. *Songwriters on Songwriting*. New York: Da Capo Press. 1997.
A wide cross-section of contemporary songwriters (Bob Dylan, Randy Newman, Brian Wilson, Jackson Browne, Neil Young, and many, many more) are interviewed here by a songwriter. Filled with great stories and insights.

Nuts-and-Bolts Business

Freund, James C. *Smart Negotiating: How to Make Good Deals in the Real World*. New York: A Fireside Book, Simon & Schuster, 1992.
An excellent book on how to negotiate good deals.

Krasilovsky, M. William, Gross, John M., and Shemel, Sidney. *This Business of Music*. New York: Billboard Publishers Inc. 9th edition, 2003.
This Business of Music is the granddaddy of music business books. Buy a copy and start studying it today. Keep *This Business of Music* always close at hand, referring to its detailed chapters and sample contracts whenever you need to.

Songwriter's Market. Edited by Ian Bessler. Cincinnati: Writer's Digest Books, 2003.
Songwriter's Market is a second must-have book, a complete compendium, updated yearly, of music publishers and other song buyers, arranged by style and their receptivity to new writers.

Publications

American Songwriter
    1009 17th Avenue South
    Nashville, TN 37212
    1-800-739-8712

Billboard
    5505 Wilshire Boulevard
    Los Angeles CA 90036

Songwriter's Market
    F & W Publications
    1507 Dana Avenue
    Cincinnati, OH 45702
    1-800-289-0963

Variety
    245 West 17th Street
    New York, NY 10011
    212-337-7001

About the Author

MICHAEL LYDON, a professional singer, songwriter, and guitarist who lives in New York, is the author of six books, including *Ray Charles: Man & Music*, a biography of the Genius. Routledge published Lydon's *Flashbacks: Eyewitness to the Rock Revolution*, in Spring 2003. A founding editor of *Rolling Stone*, Lydon has written for *The New York Times*, *Atlantic Monthly*, *Esquire*, *The Village Voice*, and is a member of ASCAP, Local 802 of the AF of M, and the faculty of the Third Street Music School Settlement.

Acknowledgments

If I thanked all the songwriters from Bach to Bacharach who've inspired me, this might be the longest section of the book. Many of my favorites found their way into the chapters, and they'll have to stand for the rest.

Many thanks to the friends who helped bring this book to life: Ellen Mandel, Peter Guralnick, Zick Rubin, Peter Lydon, Mary Lydon Fonseca, Jim Payne, Jesse Staton, Richard Carlin, and Pasquale Bianculli.

Song Permissions

"Adelaide's Lament," (from Guys and Dolls), words and music by Frank Loesser © 1950 (Renewed) Frank Music Corp. All Rights Reserved.

"Baby, It's Cold Outside," (from the motion picture Neptune's Daughter), words and music by Frank Loesser © 1948 (Renewed) Frank Music Corp. All Rights Reserved.

"Be Mine," words and music by Michael Lydon © 2004 Mopat Music (ASCAP). All rights reserved, Used by permission.

"Brush Up Your Shakespeare," words and music by Cole Porter © 1949. (Renewed) Assigned to John F. Wharton, Trustee of the Cole Porter Music & Literary Property Trusts. Publication and Allied Rights assigned to Chappell & Co. All Rights Reserved. Used by Permission. Warner Bros. Publications U.S. Inc., Miami, FL 33014.

"Embraceable You," by George Gershwin and Ira Gershwin © 1930 (Renewed) WB Music Corp. All Rights Reserved. Used by Permission. Warner Bros. Publications U.S. Inc., Miami, FL 33014.

"Foolin' Myself," by Peter Tinturin and Jack Lawrence © 1937 (Renewed) Chappell & Co. and Range Road Music Inc. All Rights outside the U.S. controlled by Chappell & Co. All Rights Reserved. Used by Permission. Warner Bros. Publications U.S. Inc., Miami, FL 33014.

"Heat Wave," words and music by Edward Holland, Lamont Dozier and Brian Holland © 1963 (Renewed 1991) Jobette Music Co., Inc. All Rights Controlled and Administered by EMI Blackwood Music Inc. on behalf of Stone Agate Music (A Division of Jobette Music Co., Inc.). All Rights Reserved International Copyright Secured. Used by Permission

"Bo Diddley," words and music by Ellas McDaniel. Copyright © 1955 (Renewed) by Arc Music Corporation (BMI). International Copyright Secured. All Rights Reserved. Used by Permission

Song Index

General Index